Under the
Banyan Tree

Under the Banyan Tree

Overcoming fear and sorrow

Thich Nhat Hanh

FULL
CIRCLE

UNDER THE BANYAN TREE
© 2008 by Unified Buddhist Church
First World Edition, September 2008
ISBN 81-7621-175-3

Transcription by Mary Therese
Edited by Anita Raina Thapan
Sketches by Priyanka Malhotra

Published by **FULL CIRCLE** *PUBLISHING*
J-40, Jorbagh Lane, New Delhi-110003
Tel: 24620063, 24621011 • Fax: 24645795
or Post Box No. 3005, Lodhi Road Post Office, New Delhi-110003
E-mail: fullcircle@vsnl.com • *website:* www.atfullcircle.com

Print & typesetting : SCANSET
J-40, Jorbagh Lane, New Delhi-110003
Printed at International Print-O-Pac Limited, Noida (U.P.), India
PRINTED IN INDIA
08/08/01/09/21/SCANSET/DE/IPP/IPP

CONTENTS

FOREWORD

A group of us sat in meditation on the beach in Chennai. Watching the sun rise, we felt we were awakening to a new dawn. This was just another ordinary day. Witnessed with an extraordinary view, this ordinary day became extraordinary. We experienced an expanded sense of mind and self, that allowed us to experience a sense of interconnectedness with each other and nature. This view, shared with us by Zen Master Thich Nhat Hanh (called "Thay" by his students), helped us touch the miracle in everything we did, whether we were walking, eating, or just breathing. These are acts we take for granted, and yet when we do them in mindfulness, they offer us an ability to touch a deeper sense of reality, both in ourselves and the world outside. That morning we felt a sense of peace and freedom that we do not often experience.

Three hundred of us had come from all over India and the rest of the world to be on a retreat at the Theosophical Society in Chennai. During the retreat, we would often visit the magnificient, spreading banyan tree in the gardens of the Society. It was under the shade of such a tree that the Buddha had renounced the path of austerity and abnegation by accepting kheer (rice milk) from Sujata.

During the retreat, it seemed to me that the banyan tree symbolises Buddhism today; the central trunk that was its core no longer asserts itself. It has passsed its strength to its aerial roots spreading all over the world.

This book is based on the teachings offered by Thay during that retreat in 1997 in Chennai. It guides us from basic practices of mindfulness meditation to deeper teachings of interdependance to insights into birth and death. More than philosophical teachings, these talks offer us a guide to living everyday in a meaningful way.

After attending a retreat for artists with Thay in the US, I had the good fortune of organising his visit 'In the Footsteps of the Buddha' in 1988. He guided thirty of us with great skill to build a relationship with the historical Buddha - the human being, see how his teachings were relevant to our lives today and to realise the Buddha (awakened mind) within ourselves.

For me, being brought up in India, "in the land of Gods," it was wonderful to tread a spiritual path that emphasised practice rather than blind faith. Since then, I have visited his growing centre, Plum Village in south west France every year and it became my home for a time. I was married there in 1996.

Thay kindly agreed to the invitation from our Ahimsa Trust to come to India again in 1997. The programme included events in Delhi, Kolkata, Chennai and the Buddhist sites of Bodh Gaya and Rajgir. He was accompanied by his long time Dharma sister, Sister Chan Khong and a group of young monks and nuns and lay practitioners.

During his visit to Delhi, he also met Mr K.R. Narayanan (then the Vice President) and had a wonderful discussion on the state of politics and soon after, the Vice President announced the formation of the Ethics Committee in the Rajya sabha. As they were introduced Thay thanked the Vice President for sparing time in his very busy schedule (it was the opening day of the budget session) and Mr. Narayanan responded by saying he would always have time for Buddhist monks.

At the time, we were keen that Thay's books could be made available to readers in India. After speaking to Shekhar and Poonam Malhotra of Hind Pocket books we felt we had found our publisher in India. In fact after reading the books we were offering for translation, the publishers decided to start a new imprint, Full Circle, and this imprint has provided a great service in exposing Thay to the larger Indian audience.

Now, as Thay returns to India after nearly 12 years, as a 'Distinguished Visitor' of the Government of India, I am glad that the teachings from the last visit are being made available. Since his visit in 1997, a small sangha of practitioners started meeting together on a regular basis. This group of friends under Ahimsa Trust are puttting together the current visit where he will be delivering the Gandhi memorial lecture, holding a national workshop for teachers, speaking to the corporate sector, doctors, dalits, social activists and many more. We hope this opportunity will bring peace and joy to those who come in contact with Thay and the monks and nun travelling with him.

Dharmacharya Shantum Seth

CHAPTER 1

LIVING IN THE PRESENT MOMENT

If you want to live, live in the present moment. If you want the Buddha it must be in the present moment. If you want *nirvana*, it has to be in the present moment. The present moment is the only one when these things are available to you. Why do you continue to run? *Samatha* means stopping and touching deeply the present moment. The present moment contains all the wonders of life, including the blue sky, including the sunshine, the tangerine and the person who is good, be it you.

When you practice walking meditation, you practice arriving in the present moment all the time because walking meditation means to walk without any intention to arrive. There is no destination. In fact, it helps you to stop running. When we go somewhere, when we walk, we have an ideal, we have a desire to arrive. When we drive, too, we have a desire to arrive. When we make a journey, only the point of arrival is considered to be of consequence. Going or moving and the moment of driving or walking is less important. That is a big mistake.

Walking meditation is a wonderful way to learn to stop and to enjoy every step you take. With some training you will be able to walk as if you were walking in paradise, in a pure land, in *nirvana*. This is possible because, according to the teaching of the Buddha, the pure land or *nirvana* is available in the present moment. You need not die in order to enter *nirvana*. In fact, you have to be really alive to do so.

If you breathe in and out mindfully, if you restore yourself completely then and only then can you pass into *nirvana* in the here and the now.

When you are able to establish yourself in the present moment, you will discover that conditions for your happiness are already there, more than enough for you to be happy. There is no need for you to run. The one who has peace, the one who has happiness, is the one who has stopped. I have stopped. I am not running behind anything else. Conditions for your happiness, you can touch them. You can recognize them, if you really are in the present moment. Suppose you practice this very simple breathing exercise:

Breathing in, I am aware of my eyes,
Breathing out I smile through my eyes.

You are practicing touching your eyes, not with your fingers, but with your mind. Mindfulness is touching your eyes.

Breathing in I am aware of my eyes,
Breathing out I smile through my eyes.

Why do we do that? When we become aware of our eyes then we are mindful of our eyes. When we are concentrating on our eyes, we find out very soon that we still have eyes in good condition. And it is a wonderful thing to have eyes that are still in good condition. It is a very basic condition for your happiness and for your peace. Those of us who have lost our eyesight, they cannot see anything. And it is their deepest desire to recover the capacity of seeing. They tell us that if they could see things again then it would be like going back to paradise. It is true. The paradise of forms and colours is wonderful. You need only sit down and open your eyes and look and breathe mindfully in order to be in paradise, in that paradise of forms and colours.

Those eyes still in good condition, those forms and colours around you that you can perceive with your good eyes, they belong to the reality that you are socially part of. They are conditions for your happiness. These conditions you do not have to find. You do not have to look for them. They are already available to you. Your eyes are in good condition, and the blue sky and the beautiful sunset and all the flowers that are blooming in this very moment, these are factors of your happiness that you can touch and recognize, if you go back to the present moment.

Breathing in I am aware of my heart,
Breathing out I smile through my heart.
I embrace my heart with the energy of mindfulness.

Maybe among us there is someone who has never paid attention to his heart before. Our heart is a miracle. When I go back to my heart and touch it daily with my mindfulness, I recognize that to have a heart that still functions normally is a real miracle. There are those that do not have that kind of happiness, they do not have a heart that functions normally. They are subjected to the danger of a heart attack or a stroke. And all of them desire to have a heart like ours, the heart that functions normally.

When we touch our heart with mindfulness, we see the fact that our heart works day and night non-stop in order to preserve our well being. One of the basic conditions for our well being and happiness is our heart. We ourselves, we have time to rest, to sleep, but not so our heart. It functions non-stop. And that is the kind of insight you develop when you practice mindfulness on the presence of your heart. Suddenly compassion arises: "Oh! my dear heart, you work so hard and yet I did not know how to take good care of you. I drink, I smoke, I eat in such a way that gives you a hard time!"

Yes, that is true, that is part of our insight. We have drunk, we have eaten, we have worked, we have lived in such a way that we have made it very hard for our heart. So out of that mindfulness, out of that insight, love is born and you decide what to do and what not to do, in order to preserve the wellbeing of your heart. That is true meditation.

Enlightenment is always enlightenment about something. Let us not be abstract. I am mindful about the fact that my heart works hard and needs my support and love. I am enlightened about how to live my daily life so that my heart will have an easy time because the well being of my heart is my whole well being. When you smoke a cigarette with mindfulness — "Smoking I am aware that I am smoking" — and if you practice mindfulness of smoking, you will stop very soon. That is called smoking meditation.

Or, when you drink your whisky in mindfulness it is called whisky meditation.

I don't say you have to stop smoking and drinking before I can give you instructions about how to meditate. I don't do that. Instead, I say: "Yes, you can begin by smoking mindfully and drinking mindfully because I know if you really do it, you will stop smoking and drinking very soon."

Every time you light up a cigarette, you commit an unfriendly act vis-a-vis your heart and your lungs. That is not the practice of love. And the Buddha taught us, "Unless you know how to take care of yourself, unless you know how to love yourself, you cannot love someone else. The love for others depends on your capacity of loving yourself. Taking care of your body, taking care of your feelings, taking care of your pain, your distress is the practice of compassion, of love."

We know that within the territory of our person there is a lot of damage that has been made by ourselves. We have done damage to our body, to our feelings, perceptions, and consciousness. We know there are a lot of conflicts within. There is a lot of war, a lot of pain within. And listening to the voice of the Buddha we have to go home and take care of the situation at home. And it is exactly with the image of mindfulness that you can go home without being afraid, because with the image of mindfulness we are able to embrace our pain, our sorrow. And we can survive. Embracing our pain our sorrow we can calm them down. And if we continue, we will be able to transform them into other forms of energies.

CHAPTER 2

OVERCOMING
FEAR AND
SORROW

The Buddha advises his monks on the five contemplations.

I am of the nature to get old. I cannot avoid old age.

That is the first contemplation. We are all afraid of getting old. We don't want to think that. We want that fear to stay down peacefully there.

I am of the nature to die. I cannot escape death.

This is the second contemplation. My fear must come up here so that I can look at it directly and the energy with which I look at it is my mindfulness.

I am of the nature to get sick. I cannot escape sickness.

That is the third contemplation.

Everything that I cherish today, I will have to leave behind tomorrow, whether it is my house, my bank account, my children or my beautiful partner. Everything that I cherish today, I will have to abandon it. I cannot carry anything with me the moment I die.

This is the fourth contemplation.

There are true facts, simple facts that you don't want to face. You want them to get lost here because you are afraid. It is painful for you to look deeper.

I am the sum of my actions, *karma*. I am only the outcome of what I have done, of what I have said, of what I have thought. These are the only things I will bring with me.

This is the fifth contemplation.

So the monks are supposed to practice this every day. Invite your fear up, smile through it and every time you smile through your fear, it will lose some of it's strength.

Looking deeply into the nature of your *dukha* and your pain is what the Buddha recommended. If you try to run away from your pain, there is no way that you can find a way out. It is by looking deeply into the very nature of suffering that you can get the way out. *Dukha*, the first noble truth, the holy truth, is the key. *Dukha* is considered to be holy because it is exactly by looking into it that you can find the form of peace, namely, the *marga* or the way out. That is why you should go back to your pain and look into it in terms of nutriments. This is a teaching of the Buddha.

There are four kinds of truth and four kinds of nutriments that must be identified if you want to end your depression or your suffering. You have to look into your suffering and identify the source of nutriment that has brought it about. If you are too old, if you cannot relate to people, if you feel cut off and want to end that kind of suffering you have to look into it in terms of nutriments. What is it in the last four or five years of your life that has made this suffering possible? This is exactly what the Buddha said. If you look deeply into what has come about and identify the source of nutriment that has got in, you are already on the path of emancipation.

Let us take the example of your depression. You are afraid of your depression. You want it to go away. What has come to be is your depression. You have to look deeply into it and identify the source of nutriments that has brought it in. This is called deep looking, *vipassana*.

The Buddha said, please remember I only teach about suffering and the way of suffering. I don't teach the way to run away from suffering because you cannot run away. Wherever you go, it will go with you.

The Buddha said the first source of nutriment is edible food. What you drink and you eat in your daily life can bring toxins into you. So you have to practice mindful eating. In the five contemplations you identify that sentence. I determine to eat only the kind of food that is nourishing and that can prevent illness. It means that I don't eat the kind of food that can bring toxins and cause a lot of pain within my body. This is what the Buddha said about edible food.

Here is a very strong image: a young couple decided to cross the desert with their little baby boy. They brought water and food in order to be able to survive the trip. But they miscalculated. Halfway through the desert they ran out of food and they knew that they were going to die, all three of them. So after much debate, the young couple decided to kill the little boy to eat his flesh. They killed him and ate a small piece and dried the rest of his flesh on their shoulders while walking. Thanks to that they crossed the desert and they survived.

The Buddha turned to his monks and said that 'Dear friends, do you think that the young couple enjoyed eating their son's flesh?" They said, "No it's impossible to enjoy eating the flesh of one's own child." The Buddha says yes, what you say there is true. We have to practice mindful eating. We should eat in such a way that compassion can be preserved in us. We should eat in such a way that can preserve life. If compassion dies out inside us, there is no way in which we can be happy.

Compassion is the only kind of energy that can help us relate to the world outside, to other living beings. Without compassion and understanding there is no way that you can be happy. You would be completely cut off, completely isolated from the world. So eat in such a way that it does not destroy the amount of compassion that is still in us. Every living being is a son or daughter to us.

When you drink a glass of liquor with mindfulness, you may get the insight that the glass of liquor has been made with a lot of grains. When you eat a piece of meat, in mindfulness, you will realize that in order to have that piece of meat the farmer had to feed the animal with so much grain while countless people in the world are dying everyday just because they don't have grains to eat. The scientists in France said that if the world reduced the eating of meat and the drinking of alcohol by 50% that would be enough to transform the face of the world. It would solve the problem of hunger.

According to UNESCO, everyday about 40,000 children die because of the lack of nutrition, because of hunger. When we drink liquor, when we eat our piece of meat in mindfulness, we are really eating the flesh of our baby boy, and we are not cultivating the energy of compassion within us. How can we be happy living in such a way? This is the image the Buddha proposes for mindful eating.

The day we flew from Paris to New Delhi, we were so happy because there was a strike and everyone on the Air France flight had to eat simple vegetables. That was a non- smoking flight and one where everyone had to eat vegetables. It was very rare. And I am so glad walking around the slum areas here where I see that even if the people are poor there is no exhibition of meat. So many people are vegetarian in India. This makes us very happy. Walking around and noticing that can bring us a lot of happiness. There is evidently some insight that has been transmitted from generation to generation in order for vegetarianism to continue to survive.

The second set of nutriments is the sense impressions, *sparsha*. What we receive by the way of the eye, what we receive by the way of the ears, what we see, what we hear, constitute the second source of nutriment. When you watch television, when you read novels, when you listen to music and conversations, you might be getting toxins and poisons into your consciousness. An article in the newspaper might contain a lot of toxins. It may nourish more violence and hatred in you. A movie can be also very toxic. I have spoken about the self-intoxication that we practice and we let our children practice everyday. We have to guard our six senses and the agent that helps us guard our six senses is mindfulness: mindfulness of looking, mindfulness of listening, mindfulness of consuming the so-called contra items. If depression is there in us and refuses to go away it is because we have fed it for the last so many months or years, with this kind of nutriment. We have listened to such types of sounds. We have viewed such types of forms. We have ingested into our consciousness the kind of toxins that make possible the depression today.

Meditation, first of all, is to look deeply and identify the source of nutriment that has brought about the pain that you have. And you can seek the help of other brothers and sisters living in the community, in the home, in the moment when you recognize the source of nutriment that has brought about your depression. You need only to cut that source of nutriment and your depression begins right away to go away, slowly. But if you continue, it will go away completely. To stop the source of nutriment is the way out because every kind of suffering has its own source of nutriment.

Let us take the case of our friend who lost both his mother and wife in the course of fifteen days and who is feeling very anxious about his daughter who is now motherless. When we look deeply we see the positive elements within us and around us. We have to recognize them, to recognize their presence for our own happiness and for the sake of maintaining these elements of mindfulness.

Of course life is impermanent. Anything can happen. There is a feeling of insecurity that is always there. My beloved one is alive today but who knows what happens to her or to him tomorrow. Things are impermanent and it cannot be sure that things that are there today will be there tomorrow. So the feeling of insecurity is a fact in every one of us.

The French poet Victor Hugo says in his poem *A Villequiers* that man is helpless, that man can only see one end of things. The other end of things sink deeply into the unknown and that is why fear and insecurity is ever present in man. Facing insecurity what kind of attitude should you adopt? The Buddha stated it very clearly: "Be aware of impermanence and do everything you can do today, in order to make the person you love happy."

If you are mindful you recognize that there are so many things that are precious to you and you will be able to nourish yourself with these positive refreshing elements around you and inside you. If you don't do it today you will regret it tomorrow. If you love someone, if you really think she or he is crucial to your happiness then love him or her properly today. Take good care of her today. Tomorrow it may be too late. That is the wisdom. "Darling I know you

are there alive and I am very happy." You should be able
to tell him or her that. This is the practice of mindfulness,
mindfulness of what is precious to you. "Darling I know
you are there and I am very happy.'

There are moments when I look at the full moon and I
practice that. "Dear full moon I know you are there and I am
very happy." I embrace the moon with my mindfulness. I am
happy when I feel that the moon is happy also. Tomorrow I
will not have any regret. This is the answer to impermanence
and to insecurities. That is one thing we have to learn. We
suffer only when we lose things or lose people, but while
they are still around we have no capacity of recognizing
them as precious. The daughter, she is motherless but
she still has a father. And she is living with her aunt. She
should be able to appreciate the fact that although her
mother is no longer there, her aunt is there taking care
of her. And her father still lives in India as her support.
So you change your way of looking at things.

There is a tree dying in the garden. Yes that is the
truth, but you have to recognize the fact that there are
other trees that are still alive. Don't let yourself be pulled
down just because one tree has died. Do not let one mental
formation dominate everything because you are more than
one emotion. In your emotions you are capable of being
joyful or peaceful or being loving. Don't let just one thing
dominate everything. Stand up, touch the other positive

things that are in you. Become alive and you will be a source of joy and support to your daughter. Look at the Ashoka trees. Ashoka means 'no sorrow'. You have to practice like the tree. You have to practice no sorrow. No sorrow is a matter of positive mental formations in us. We have to nourish the state of no sorrow in us because the seed of joy, of peace is still there.

The Buddha offers a second very powerful image of the second source of nutriment. It is the image of a cow that has a skin disease. It does not seem to have any skin anymore. When you lead the cow close to a tree all the tiny living beings living in the bark of the tree will come out and stick to the body of the cow and suck the blood. And if you lead the cow close to the road to a path of stones and bricks, all the tiny living beings will feel the blood and will come out and stick to the body of the cow and suck. And if you lead the cow into the water all the living beings in the water will come to the body of the cow and suck. It is like this. Without mindfulness you open the doors of the six senses and you let all the toxins and impressions in. You will be invaded by them, intoxicated by them. Just drive through the city and look at the advertisements, listen to the music. There are so many toxins in them.

Without the practice of mindful living we allow toxins to come through all the six doors of our senses and that is why we have to protect ourselves. We have to be careful.

We should not become the victims of invasion by toxins, by poisons coming from every side. Learn how to look, to watch mindfully. Learn how to listen mindfully and decide not to ingest anymore toxins.

The Buddha uses another image to tell us how to embrace the pain within us. It is the image of the sunshine embracing the vegetation. Imagine that your anger or despair is like a flower and that the image of mindfulness is like the sunshine embracing the flower. In the early morning the lotus flowers, they are not yet open. They wait for the sunshine. The sunshine does not run around the flower. It tries to penetrate into the flower. We know that light is made of photons and each grain of light tries to enter into the flower. So light as a kind of energy tries to penetrate into the heart of the flower. It may take half an hour, one hour or an hour and a half. The flower may not have opened but the sunshine continues to embrace and penetrate into it. And after sometime when the energy of the sunshine is strong enough, the flower will have to open itself and show its heart to the sun.

So when we know how to embrace our pain with the energy of mindfulness, that energy of mindfulness will try to calm down the intensity of our pain. The energy of mindfulness is the second source of energy that is penetrating into the first source of energy, the energy of pain. One source of energy is embracing another source of energy. And if we know how to nourish our mindful breathing we can maintain the energy of mindfulness with us, for the embracing of the pain to continue. When we are there really caring and embracing our pain, the act of looking deeply is something that will follow. Then at some point, suddenly, we will be able to see the true nature of our pain. Then that kind of vision, that kind of insight will be liberating for us.

The energy of mindfulness has the power of calming and transforming. All vegetation is sensitive to light. The chlorophyll that the vegetation fabricates, it is from light. All vegetation is sensitive, photo-sensitive. In exactly the same way, all mental formations in us are sensitive to the energy of mindfulness. Mindfulness is like the sunshine. When it touches something it can help to make that something appear more clearly. It can calm it down and it can penetrate into the nature of that something in order for that something to reveal its true nature to us, exactly like light.

When you contemplate a tangerine with mindfulness, because of mindfulness you are really there. And mindfulness helps you to see the tangerine clearly and it helps the tangerine to reveal itself clearly to you. When you are there, looking mindfully at the beautiful sunset, the beautiful sunset will reveal itself to you clearly. And

that is the first function of mindfulness, to help you to be there and to help reveal the true nature of what is there. And then the next function of mindfulness is to calm down what is there.

The third function of mindfulness is to help you to look deeply into the nature of the insight that you get. That has a very liberating power. All mental formations are sensitive to the energy of mindfulness. That is why cultivating the energy of mindfulness in our daily life is a very crucial practice. It is with that mindfulness energy that we can transform everything for the better. And that is why people used to say that the energy of mindfulness is the energy of the Buddha or the Boddhisatva. The energy of mindfulness contains the energy of concentration, understanding and compassion. Cultivating that energy is the heart of the Buddhist practice of meditation.

The third source of nutriment is called volition, the intention, the deep desire in us, *satana*. All of us have deep desires within and it is this kind of volition that keeps us alive, a reason to be there, to continue to live. We are all motivated by some kind of desire. We have to practice looking deeply into the nature of that desire. That desire is the third kind of fruit, without it we cannot continue to live.

The Buddha also had a deep desire, that deep desire was to be free, to be enlightened, to be compassionate, to be understanding and to be able to help living beings to suffer less, that was his deep desire. Other people desire to be famous, they desire success, power. They desire to have a lot of money, a high position in society, they desire to have sex, and so on. We have to look into the nature of our desires to see whether the third kind of nutriment is bringing us a lot of sorrow and pain. In us there is a seed of desire. We desire freedom. We all want freedom and we know that freedom is a very essential element for our happiness. Without that freedom we cannot be happy at all. We seek freedom from sorrow, freedom from pain, freedom from afflictions, from jealousy, from fear and from craving.

If we suffer a lot, maybe we have in us the kind of desire that is not healthy, the kind of desire that is pushing us in the direction of suffering. That is why we have to re- examine the third source of nutriments that we feed ourselves everyday.

The Buddha uses this example: There is a person who would like to be happy. He does not want to be burned by the fire and yet he is attracted by two strong persons. They come and they carry him and they want to throw him onto a heap of burning charcoal. He doesn't want to suffer. He doesn't want to be thrown into the burning charcoal. But the two men are very strong. They forcibly carry him off and throw him into the pit of burning charcoal. This is the example the Buddha used.

The two men represent the force of the third kind of nutriment. Suppose we crave for something and think of it day and night, we get so addicted that we are carried away by the force of our craving in the direction of suffering. Craving is a form of unhealthy food. So also is jealousy, the will to revenge, the desire to be famous, wealthy, powerful, the desire to be the president of a powerful corporation, the desire to be the president, the boss. All these are described as the third kind of nutriment.

If we suffer in the present moment we should look deeply into that desire to see whether it is that kind of desire that has made us suffer. If we practice looking deeply we see that our notion of happiness may be responsible for our suffering. We believe that in order to be really happy we have to grab this or that. And we believe that if we cannot achieve this or that we cannot be really happy. Therefore we are being abducted by our volition. A whole nation can also be carried away by one desire. We believe that such an ideal is very crucial for the happiness of the whole nation, the only way for the nation to become strong and happy. Therefore, the political party would like the whole nation to follow that ideology in order to achieve happiness.

Sometimes that nation has to go through fifty or seventy years of painful experiences in order to realize that they have suffered a great deal because of that particular notion of happiness. They have suffered because people had told them that there is only one way to be happy as a nation, to follow that particular ideology , to realize it.

So sometimes we need seventy years to realize that what we had was a wrong notion. And during that time we have suffered a lot. Many people opposed to the regime have been exiled or put in mental hospitals or camps. Then, one day, because you suffer so much, you wake up and realize that your notion of happiness has been responsible for your suffering. So, each of us has an idea of happiness. And we should be able to sit down and look deeply into that idea of happiness.

If you are committed to one idea of how to be happy, that is dangerous. It may be that very idea of happiness that has prevented you from being really happy. There are many ways to be happy, but you are committed to only one way of being happy. We have to examine our desire, our notion of happiness. For a person like me, for instance, to become a prime minister of a nation is not something that is appealing at all. I think to be a monk is much better, because the life of a monk as I live it, brings me a lot of happiness. I am free. I have so much freedom as a monk.

I know that a prime minister has power, but that kind of power, I don't need. I need the power to be free, to walk mindfully and to enjoy every step I take. I need the time and the energy to help people to suffer less. I need opportunities to organise retreats and days of mindfulness in order to help people to look deeply into their situation, so that they can abandon their wrong views, their bad habits and transform themselves, so that they can smile and reconcile with their people. That brings me a lot of happiness.

I, too, have a desire but I know that the desire I have does not bring me unhappiness. *Apranihita* is a Sanskrit word. It means wishlessness. You do not put in front of you an object of desire and then run after it. You know that happiness is available in the here and the now. You recognize elements of your happiness in the here and the now. Why should you have to run after many things? And when you are able to actually enjoy happiness in the here and the now, you are desire free. And nobody can carry you into the realm of suffering. It is our desire for fame, sex, power, that carries us to the pit of burning charcoal. That is why the Buddha advises us to look again deeply into the nature of our desires. We suffer just because of them.

The fourth source of nutriment is called consciousness. We have many seeds of sorrow and pain in us and every time these seeds are touched or watered, they manifest themselves on the upper level of our consciousness. When you allow the seed of jealousy to manifest itself on the upper level of your consciousness, for example, you suffer so much and you consume that energy of jealousy, day and night. That is not healthy, to eat and to consume and to digest that kind of nutriment called jealousy. If you have a seed of anger, every time that seed is watered, it manifests in your mind consciousness and the anger burns you and you don't know how to deal with it. You let the anger remain in yourself, overwhelming you, consuming you. And everyday we consume a lot of poisons, manifested as the objects of our consciousness: fear, anger, distress, jealousy, depression and so on

The Buddha used an image to explain this very tragic state. There is one criminal in the kingdom and the king has been searching for him. One day the police reports that the criminal has been arrested and they want the king to decide upon the punishment that is to be given to him. The king says: "Bring him out and have 300 sharp knives plunged into him, going through him. Use 300 knives and stab him." After this was done, the king asked, "How is he now?" The guard replied that he was still alive.

The king said, "This afternoon bring him out and do the same thing to him using 100 sharp knives and have

these knives go through his body." In the evening he once again asked, "How is the man now?" And the guard said, "He is still alive'.

The king said, "Bring him out and repeat the punishment once more today." So after having used this kind of example, the Buddha said, "We do exactly like this. We make ourselves suffer everyday, in this manner. We suffer innumerable times and from many kinds of knives. Anger is a knife. So are hatred, jealousy and despair. We are torturing ourselves day and night just because we consume all these poisons, all these mental formations, and that is why we have to learn the way to stop these four kinds of nutriments.

When you read a magazine, listen to the radio or watch television, you might allow these kinds of mental formations to be touched and to be manifested in you, like fear, violence, distress, discrimination. You are consuming these things everyday. Only mindfulness will help you see that you are killing yourself, stabbing yourself, torturing yourself. When enlightenment comes you will know what to do in order to stop that kind of auto-intoxication.

The Buddha said, "What has come to be, if you know how to look into its nature, and identify the source of nutriments, you are already on the path of emancipation." And that is why right view, right insight is the capacity to identify the source of nutriment that has brought about the pain that you are undergoing. *Samadrishti* — right view — is the definition of this practice by the Buddha himself.

The five wonderful precepts, *shilas*, are a very wonderful way of protecting ourselves from ingesting toxins and poisons into our consciousness. And a person who lives according to the five wonderful precepts is someone who is protecting herself / himself and his family from the invasions of these poisons. And if we know how to protect ourselves we will be able to cut the source of nutriments that have brought in many of the sufferings that we have to undergo.

CHAPTER 3

RESTORING
COMMUNICATION

In order to restore communication, you have to learn the art of listening very deeply and using loving speech. In our times telecommunication and other sophisticated technology can help us to communicate very easily. It needs no time at all to communicate our ideas and facts to other parts of the world. But it is in this very time that communication has become very difficult between men, men and women, father and son/daughter, husband and wife. In many families, although they live together under one roof, they cannot really communicate. They live as though in a guest house, in a hotel.

I remember the French writer, Antoine de Saint Exupery who says, "To love each other is not to look at each other, but to look in one direction." There is some truth in that. When we love each other, we share the same ideas. I find it amazing how many people in a family cannot bear to look at each other. It is not pleasant anymore. In the beginning they say, "Without you I cannot survive." Yes, that is true at the start, but because they are not very skilful, not mindful in their daily lives, they create for each other a lot of *samyojanas* or internal knots. Then it becomes unpleasant to look at the other person. Instead it feels better to look in the direction of the television.

That is the situation in many families. We don't look at each other anymore. We only look at the television in order to suffer less. That is a tragedy. Having lost the capacity to communicate, we are not able anymore to listen to each other, because when we speak we are not able to speak normal speech. We let our anger, frustration, bitterness and pain spill all over the other person who does not find it pleasant to listen to you.

So you feel that no one understands you. It is impossible to communicate because no one around has the capacity to listen to you and at that very time your pain is so great. I know of many families where the husband cannot talk to or cannot listen to his wife. Children cannot listen to parents and each of them live in very different worlds. And when you have no way to express your pain, your difficulties, you can no longer bear that kind of suffering and you become insane. Then with some mental illness you have to look for a psycho-therapist. Who is that person, the psycho-therapist?

The psycho-therapist is the one who accepts to sit down and to listen to you. But you have to pay him or her. That is very expensive. Since no one in your family is able to listen to you, you have to look for a psycho-therapist. You have the right to talk and it is his or her duty to listen to you. That is why there are so many therapists in our society. I have offered several retreats for psycho-therapists in the west. About 500 to 600 psycho-therapists have attended them. I know of psycho-therapists who suffer very deeply. Many cannot talk to their partners, their children. Eventually they

have to tell the truth to the teacher because they themselves need help.

The pain in them is also very great and if you have to bear the pain within yourself, it is difficult for you to listen to the pain of another person. And the most important quality of a psycho-therapist is the ability to listen. In Buddhism we talk about that Boddhisattva who has the capacity to listen. In Buddhism we talk about Avalokiteshvara, the Boddhisattva who has the capacity to listen deeply to the sounds of the world. Avalokita is capable of sitting down and listening to you. And even if you say wrong things he is still able to listen because the quality of his listening is high, because he knows how to nourish compassion in himself while listening to you. This practice is called compassionate listening.

If you want to help your beloved one, to make him/her suffer less you have to learn the art of compassionate listening. You have to train yourself, so that for the whole time of sitting and listening, compassion should be maintained and nourished. You breathe in and breathe out mindfully and always remember that you are listening to him/her not for judging, not for criticizing, but just for one purpose: to give him a chance to speak out and to suffer less.

You are sitting very calmly. Your eyes translate compassion in you. Your ears translate the willingness to listen, you breathe in and breathe out. You remind yourself all the time, "I listen in order to help him suffer less, and for no other purpose." If you can nourish that kind of compassion and understanding in you, even if the other person accuses you, even if the other person says many wrong things yet you remain calm, listening intensively and with compassion.

If you can sit and listen like that for one hour, it will be very heavy. You have to play the role of a Boddhisattva. You cannot expect someone else to do it for you because you know the other person better than anyone else. If you have time to breathe and to look deeply, you will understand that he is only suffering and you will understand your part of responsibility in the making of that suffering. Then you can go to him and tell him/her in the language of enlightenment, "My dear friend you have suffered quite a lot in the past many years. I am not blind. I have seen it. I suffer also when I see you suffer and I have been stupid. I have made so many mistakes. I have reacted angrily. I have spoken with much bitterness and I have caused your anger and suffering to grow all the time. Now I realize that and I really feel sorry. I don't want you to continue like that. I want you to help me, so that I will not continue to make you suffer. Please tell me my mistake. Please tell me of your suffering and your pain. I am really eager to listen."

If you can use that kind of language, the other person might start to cry, because you have not been able to use that kind of language for a long time. Now, thanks to the practice, thanks to the understanding and the enlightenment you have got, you are capable of being compassionate. You are capable of using this loving way of speaking. If that person begins to cry, you know that his heart is open once more to you. You have to be careful. This may be your last chance. Sit very quietly and continue to breathe in and out and listen. And from time to time you say "Oh I am sorry, my dear, please tell me more", and you help him/her to empty his heart.

I know a lady who lives in California. Her husband was that type of person that could be compared to the bomb. She suffered so much. The children were grown up and everyone in her family has got a PhD degree but that is not paradise. Everyone suffered. It was hell. No communication was possible between them and the lady had contemplated suicide several times. Now she had a friend who is a Buddhist practitioner and one day that friend offered her a tape in which was recorded one *dharma* talk of mine on the theme of diffusing the bomb. This unhappy lady, being a Catholic, did not want anything to do with Buddhism. "Why should I listen to this Buddhist stuff?" She asked. So she refused.

She had not committed suicide because there was still within her one seed of reason. She still had a brother who was living in a communist country and she was trying her best to get him to come to America. That way they could lean on each other, to continue to survive because she was really lonely, very alone in the world. She did not get any comfort from her husband and her children. One day she learnt that her brother was able to leave the communist country and come to her. At the airport they cried and she thought that now it would be possible for her to survive because of the presence of her brother. The happiness, however, did not last long. Just six months later they had a dispute and she told to go away. "You are not my brother, go away", she said. And this time she really wanted to kill herself.

She telephoned her Buddhist friend who pleaded with her, "Wait, take a taxi and come here". The friend persuaded her this time to listen to the *dharma* talk. The talk was for the duration of an hour and a half and it was about diffusing a bomb. It was about how much responsibility you have in the making of a difficult situation. Strangely enough, while listening to the *dharma* talk, this unhappy lady got the insight that she was responsible to a very high degree for creating the situation of suffering. She cried a lot while listening to the tape and after that she told her friend that she would go home and try to practice by helping diffuse the bomb in her husband.

The other lady, however, said, "No, my dear friend. You are not strong enough to do that. You need to practice for some time before you can practice listening deeply and using loving speech. Otherwise you will get angry again very easily, because the bomb in you is also quite big. My teacher is coming from Europe. He will be offering a few retreats in the area. Why don't you sign up for a retreat like that to practice? After that you might go home and try."

So she signed up for that retreat and learnt the art of silent walking, mindful breathing, compassionate breathing. There were six days of training and she did it because for her it was a matter of life and death. After that she went home in a very peaceful state of mind and told her husband that she wanted to begin anew, that she had made him suffer a lot and that she wanted relief for both of them. That she was very successful in her practice is evident because she could convince him to come for the next retreat organised in the area.

We did not know about this story until very much later. On the fifth day of the second retreat, her husband stood up during the team meditation session and he introduced his wife to us. He said, "My dear brothers and sisters in the *dharma*, I would like to introduce to you this wonderful Boddhisattva who is my wife. She has done everything she could do in order to make me happy, but I did not

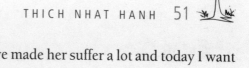

recognize that. I have made her suffer a lot and today I want to officially apologize in front of all of you." That was the couple I was talking about.

A few weeks later when we organised a day of mindfulness at the Spirit Rock Meditation Centre in Northern California, both of them came again with their three children. The *dharma* talk did touch their hearts and it is because of the practice of looking deeply, of compassionate listening, that they could restore communication between each other and become a happy family again.

I think that all of us have to train ourselves in the art of compassionate listening. The systems with which you can practice compassionate listening is mindfulness. We have to learn to listen again. With a fair amount of understanding we can nourish our compassion during the time we sit and listen. It is very healing. It can restore communication. As far as loving speech is concerned we also need to practice cultivating the energy of mindfulness. If you know how to breathe in and out and calm you body and emotions, you will be able to speak calmly. And every time you see some irritation coming up, you should refrain from talking.

There is a practice called 'beginning anew' that I would like to share with you. It can be practiced at home, in France, at Plum Village, we practice it every week. Everyone sits in a circle with a vase with one flower in the center. If there is only joy and happiness in the community then we only practice what we call 'flower watering'.

You bow to the community, you ask for the right to speak and you walk slowly to the centre of the circle. You take the flower, you go back to your seat and you sit down. You are the only one who has the right to speak. All the others only have the right to listen. Flower watering is to look at one person and discover all the positive qualities of that person and speak about them. When I water the positive seeds in him, these seeds will grow and will make him happy and with the attention of other people in the community, with the mindfulness of everyone, these seeds will grow very quickly and inspire more confidence and self esteem.

You can continue to water the flowers of the other members of the community or family. If there is one person who suffers in the family then we allow him or her to have a chance to speak out. That person alone has the right to speak. She has the right to say anything that is in her heart and everyone else practices compassionate listening. It means that even if that person is saying things that are not correct, is making remarks based on wrong perceptions, you still sit very quietly, breathing, smiling and listening with compassion. That kind of listening is very healing.

After the person finishes speaking, you allow time and space for her to heal, even if she has said many wrong things. One week later you may come to her personally and say, "The other day we listened to you deeply. I am sorry that you suffer so much. There are many things you said, I did not know, but I think there is one thing I can help you to see more correctly. You said something that is borne from some misunderstanding", and you try to help her to see correctly with loving kindness. That is the way you help the person to correct his or her wrong perceptions and not to dispute or to challenge them in a meeting.

In that session of deep listening you don't reply, you don't answer, you don't comment. You just listen. You have a purpose: to listen in order to alleviate the pain of the other person. It is very important for children, for young people. We have to give them a chance. There are children who bear suffering for a long time and who do not have a chance to speak it out. As for the person who practices this strictly, he or she has to train himself also. When you feel that there is some irritation coming up, you should not say anything: "Please, dear one, allow me to breathe for a few minutes before I continue". And you breathe so that you can restore your perfect calm before you continue. If you try hard and still cannot become calm then you say, "Sorry, my friend, today I cannot do it. Please allow me another chance."

You can say everything in your heart provided that you use loving speech with calmness. I think that is a good tradition to be established in family life. The practice of loving speech and the practice of looking deeply are the only true practices that can restore communication. In our world, the modern world, communication seems to be too difficult. No one tries to listen to anyone.

About two weeks ago I had a chance to meet with the Vice-President of India. In our conversation we talked about politics and meditation. Since he is responsible for the parliament, we discussed the art of loving speech and deep listening to be practiced in the parliament. I proposed to him that a short text be written out to be read in the beginning of each session, something of just three or four lines. It could be something like this: "The people who have elected us expect that we listen deeply to each other, to understand the viewpoint of others and to use only calm loving speech with each other so that communication can be possible. The well-being of the country and of the people depends on our capacity of speaking and listening to each other as representatives of the people. Let us practice this during this session."

I think such ideas should be accepted by all people. Regardless of the spiritual or religious traditions that we may belong to, we should recognize the necessity of listening deeply, with compassion, and using only loving speech. In the parliament, almost all the time, they shout at each other with anger and they don't really listen. They cannot represent us like that. We expect them to be able to listen to each other, to understand, because each person may have good ideas and insight, but if you cannot understand, cannot listen, how can you be receptive to his or her view? I also proposed something like this, that every time the atmosphere becomes very heated, the chairman or the president of the Congress be allowed to use the way of mindfulness. "Listen, listen, listen ……and this wonderful sound brings me back to my calm." Then he should wait until the heat dies down in order to continue with the debate. When the chairperson sees that one member of the parliament is using violent speech and insulting other members, he has the right to disrupt by saying, "Dear sir, you are asked by this assembly to speak in a calm way. You are expected to tell everything that you have in your heart, but please use calm speech. Please practice breathing, until you restore your calm before you continue.'

So that is the kind of conversation I had with the Vice-President. He was very warm. That day he had to inaugurate the first session of parliament. So in the beginning I said, "Mr. Vice-President, on a day like this when you are very busy, it is wonderful that you can have some time to meet a monk." And he said, "It is very important to me to have time to meet a monk."

I believe that not only in the family but in school, in congress, everywhere, we should learn the art of deep listening, mindful listening, compassionate listening, the art of Avalokiteshvara. We should train ourselves in the art of using loving speech, calm speech. Unless we practice like that we cannot restore good communication and without communication, there is war. Moreover, our practice is not to be cut off from the world, from reality. Our practice is to go back to the reality of our society, of our family, our community with much strength, the strength of listening deeply, the strength of using loving speech. Thus the energy of mindfulness, the insight, the compassion, cultivated in our daily lives should be able to transform our situations within our family, within the community or the congress, between different spiritual or religious communities, and between different countries.

CHAPTER 4

DISCOVERING DEATHLESSNESS

Looking deeply into this sheet of paper we can touch its nature of no birth. For to be born means from nothing you suddenly become something. This is not true concerning this sheet of paper. It did not come from nothing. You also, myself also, we have not come from nothing. We come from everything. Our true nature is no birth. The act of looking deeply, of meditating, reveals our nature of no birth. And if something has not been born, can it die? According to our habitual thinking death means that from someone you suddenly become no one. You are, and suddenly you become nothingness. That is our idea of death, from something you suddenly become nothing. From someone you suddenly become no one and we suffer very much because of this idea of ours about death.

So to meditate means looking deeply into the nature of our notion of death. Suppose now I try to make this sheet of paper into nothingness. I attempt that by using fire. I want to reduce it to nothingness. Do you think I can do it? Let us try. Anyone has a match? Please observe me to see whether we are able to reduce something into non-existence. People have tried to annihilate what or who they didn't like, for example Martin Luther King or Mahatma Gandhi. They wanted to reduce them to nothingness, but have they been successful?

If you have observed like I have, you would have noticed that the part of the sheet of paper that I set fire to has gone up in the form of smoke. It has said good bye to us, flying up to the sky and joining a cloud. The sheet of paper has changed its form of life. It has now become part of a cloud. You should look up to the sky and say, "Good bye, *salaam*" because tomorrow or the day after, while walking in the street a drop of rain might fall on your head. That is our next appointment with the sheet of paper. Perhaps in a few weeks we may step on a little flower, or a blade of grass and that small flower or blade of grass may be the continuation of the sheet of paper.

Some heat has been produced during the burning. I almost burned my finger. That energy called heat has penetrated into my body. I continue the life of the sheet of paper. You do not have an instrument sophisticated enough to measure it but that heat has also penetrated into you and you, too, continue the life of the sheet of paper. Here is some ash. The young monk here may take it out later and pour it on the grass. Who knows what will become of it in a few days or a few weeks. So the sheet of paper has gone in several directions to continue its life.

To meditate means to follow closely in order to see the coming and the going of everything that is. There is a Zen practice where the student is asked: "Tell me dear student, what did you look like before your grandmother was born?"

This is a very nice invitation for you to go and search for your true self, for your true identity. Where have you come from? You can extend that invitation to the sheet of paper. We ask the sheet of paper to go back and identify itself as a tree, as a cloud, as the sunshine. We ask the sheet of paper to go on a journey, to go and see itself as part of a cloud, a blade of grass. Nothing has been created, nothing is going to die, to become nothingness. That is our true nature, the true nature of Buddha, the true nature of all of us, the true nature of a leaf, a flower, a sheet of paper.

If we are able to remove the notion of birth and death, we can remove our fear also. There are many of us who are afraid of annihilation, afraid of non-being. Let us visualize a cloud floating in the sky. The cloud floating in the sky has a good feeling. To be a cloud and to be floating in the blue sky is a wonderful. But the cloud will become rain at any time and if the cloud is bound by his idea of life and death it will be scared. But if the cloud has the insight of no birth and no death, it will continue to enjoy itself. It will see that to be a cloud floating in the sky is wonderful, but to become rain and fall on the ground and become part of the river is also wonderful.

If that cloud has that kind of insight, the moment that it transforms into rain, it will be singing and falling at the same time. We should learn from that kind of attitude, of having no fear. Why should I be afraid of being born? Why should I be afraid of dying? Because birth and dying are only notions that cannot be applied to reality. The moment of birth is only a moment of continuation, so instead of singing "Happy birthday my dear', we have to sing 'Happy continuation day my dear.'

A French scientist, whose name is Lavosier, declared, "*Rien ne se cree, rien ne se perd.*" "Nothing is born, nothing dies." Although he did not practice as a Buddhist he used exactly the same words that have been used in the *Heart Sutra*. As a scientist, he found the same truth the Buddha discovered without ever having learnt the *Heart Sutra*. We recite this *sutra* everyday: "There is nothing that is born, nothing can die," but we only chant. We don't practice deep looking. If we knew how to practice deep looking, we would be able to remove our notion of birth and death and we would be free of fear. The notion of being and non-being are also two notions to be transcended. When conditions are sufficient, something reveals itself. Because we can perceive it, we term it as existing, as being. When something hides itself away because conditions are not sufficient then we qualify it as non-existent, as non-being.

The Buddha said that these are notions are to be removed. *Bhava* and *abhava* — existence and non-existence — are just ideas, notions. To be craving for existence or to be craving for non-existence are extremes and these kinds of attitudes are based on wrong notions, the notion of being, the notion of non-being. The one who has the insight is not caught by the notion of being. Nor is he caught by the notion of non-being because being and non-being both cannot reveal the truth. They cannot be applied to the truth. It is like our notion of above and below. We are sitting here and we are quite sure that this direction is our above and this direction is our below. Now just visualize our German brothers and sisters in the *dharma* who are practicing sitting meditation on the other side of the planet. They are sitting something like upside down and this is the way to be above, their above is the below and what we believe to be our below is their above. So the idea of above and below cannot be applied to the cosmos. Likewise the idea of birth and death cannot be applied to reality, to the outer reality. The notion of being and non-being cannot be applied to life. That is why we can say, "To be or not to be, that is not the question." The question is whether we can touch the nature of inter being.

The Buddha had a lay disciple named Anathapindika. It is that lay person who had offered the Buddha the Jeta Grove in the city of Sravasti after the enlightenment of the Buddha. It was the King Bimbisara who had offered the first monastery for the Buddha, the Bamboo Grove, near the city of Rajagriha. The second piece of land offered to the Buddhist *sangha* was the Jeta Grove and the lay person who offered it to the Buddha was Anathapindika. According to what I learnt from the *sutra*, Anathapindika was a very happy lay person because his practice was according to the teaching of the Buddha. The first time he heard the word' Buddha' he was very excited. He exclaimed: "Buddha, who is the Buddha? What a wonderful name!" The term 'Buddha' means a person who is awake.

A few hours later Anathapindika was able to make acquaintance with the Buddha and he became one of his dearest lay disciples. He spent many years serving the Buddha and the *sangha* and derived a lot of happiness by doing so. He practiced the five wonderful precepts. His wife and his three children also received the five precepts of the training and practiced as lay members of the *sangha*.

One day while staying in the Jeta Grove, the Buddha learnt that Anathapindika was very sick and dying. So he paid a visit to Anathapindika and after that asked his disciple Sariputra to take care of him. Sariputra was one of the most intelligent disciples of the Buddha. He was a big brother of many monks and nuns and it is he who first went with Anathapindika to the city of Sravasti in order to prepare the ground for the Buddha to come and teach in the kingdom of Kosala. That is why Anathapindika and Sariputra were very close friends. One was a monk and the other a layperson. I hope that every monk has a friend like Anathapindika and I hope that every lay person has a friend like Sariputra. They supported each other so well. And that is why the Buddha entrusted Anathapindika to Sariputra.

So Sariputra came and visited Anathapindika every three days. Then, one day he learnt that Anathapindika was dying. So he asked his younger brother in the *sangha*, the venerable Ananda, to come along with him. When they arrived, Anathapindika tried his best to sit up to welcome the monks but was too weak to do so. Sariputra said, "Dear friend, don't worry, please be rested. We will bring a few chairs and sit close to you." Then when they were seated Sariputra asked, "My dear friend, how do you feel within your body? Is the pain in your body increasing or decreasing?"

Anathapindika said, "Venerables, the pain in me is increasing all the time. I suffer too much." When Sariputra heard that, he decided to offer Anathapindika a few exercises in guided meditation. He said, "Dear friend, let us practice the recollection of the Buddha, the recollection of the *dharma*, and the recollection of the *sangha*, the *Buddha-anusmarati, dharma-anusmarati, sangha-anusmarati.*

He decided to use this exercise because he knew very well that focusing Anathapindika's mind on the Buddha, on the *dharma* and on the *sangha*, would bring a lot of happiness to him, because he had spent so much time serving the Buddha, the *dharma* and the *sangha*. That, in fact, did happen because after a few minutes of mindfulness, breathing with the object of the Buddha, the *dharma* and the *sangha*, Anathapindika restored his balance and began to suffer less. With the two monks sitting there, guiding him, supporting him, he felt a decrease in the pain within his body and he began to smile. At that time Sariputra asked him to practice mindfulness on the elements of his body. "Dear friend, let us practice together, you and both of us, the three of us:

These eyes are not me, I am not caught by these eyes
These ears are not me, I am not caught by these ears
This body is not me, I am not caught by this body
I am life without boundaries
My eyes are not me, what my eyes see, is not me either.

In this manner he continued to guide Anathapindika so that the latter would not identify himself with his body, with what he was seeing, in order to reveal to him his true nature of no birth and no death. If you are dying with the idea that you are this body, then it will be very painful. You will be the victim of fear. That is why it is very important to look deeply in order to disassociate yourself from this body and everything that is impermanent. Finally, they arrived at the moment when they practiced the emptiness of the body. The body, when conditions are sufficient, reveals itself. The body has not come from anywhere. When conditions are no longer sufficient, the body ceases to be perceived. The body does not go anywhere.

They practiced looking into the nature of no coming, no going of the body. The body when conditions are sufficient, reveals itself. We cannot qualify it as being. The body after disintegration, because of the lack of conditions, can no longer be perceived. We cannot qualify it as non-being. "Dear friend, dear Anathapindika everything is empty of a separate self, everything is free from birth and death, being and non-being." Thus through successive exercises of guided meditation, Sariputra showed to Anathapindika that his true nature is the nature of no birth and no death and made it possible for non-fear to be born in his person.

When Anathapindika practiced to that point he began to cry. Tears were running down his cheeks and the venerable Ananda said: "Dear friend, why are you crying? Do you regret something? Or don't you succeed in the practice of this guided meditation?"

You know that Ananda was younger than Sariputra and less experienced than him. He was a little worried about Anathapindika but, in fact, Anathapindika was very successful. He said: "Dear venerable Ananda, no I don't regret anything and my practice is very successful. I cry because I am so moved. In the 30 — 35 years I served the

Buddha, I learnt quite a lot but I have never tasted the practice such as the one that has been given to me by the venerable Sariputra. I am so moved. I am so happy, it is liberating me. I feel fine, I feel joyful within myself."

Ananda said: "Dear friend, you don't know, but we monks and nuns receive this kind of teaching almost everyday." Again Ananda was still young and upon that declaration by Ananda, the lay person Anathapindika said, 'Lord Ananda, please go home and tell the Lord Buddha that we lay people, many of us are able to receive such wonderful teachings and practice. There are those of us who are caught in wealth, fame, power, who have no capacity of receiving and practicing such a great teaching. But there are others, like myself, who are free enough to receive these teachings and we can successfully practice them."

Those were the last words of Anathapindika because after having made that declaration, he sank into a coma. The venerables left and a few hours later, the people in the family of Anathapindika informed the monks that he had died very peacefully and happily, with a smile on his lips.

The *sutra* that contains all this information is available in Pali and in Chinese. Of course it has been translated into English. I have here the English text that I translated from the Chinese. You can ask to have a copy of this *sutra*. It is only three pages long. I think we have to do like

Anathapindika. We have to have a chance to learn this wonderful teaching of the Buddha about no birth, no death, no being, no non-being, in order to get rid of our notions, in order to make non-fear arrive in us. For, it is only when you have non-fear in you, that you get the greatest release. Nirvana means extinction, blowing out. Extinction, first of all, means the extinction of all notions and ideas.

I would like to go back briefly to the case of our friend who lost his mother and his wife in just fifteen days of each other and who is worried about his daughter who is now motherless and who now lives with her aunt. Our friend is overwhelmed by grief, sorrow and worries. He keeps thinking that his daughter is alone, motherless and he doesn't have any joy for his daily living. With some practice of mindfulness he will be able to look deeply again. His daughter, although she is motherless, still has a father. That is something. Many people, many young children have neither a mother nor a father. That daughter of his has an aunt because the sister of our friend is taking care of his daughter. And who is that sister of his? She is the continuation of his mother. "It is fortunate that I still have a sister alive and who is that sister of mine? She is the continuation of my mother. I just look at her and I see my mother. And I am also the continuation of my mother. If I look deeply I can still feel the presence of my mother in me and in my sister and also in my daughter."

Our sorrow is born just because we don't know how to look deeply. There are many conditions for our happiness and well-being. We should not ignore them just because we have one feeling of sorrow. My friend may lie down, may sit down practicing deep looking and begin to write his daughter a letter. "My dear little daughter, do you know something? You are the continuation of your mother. Every time I see you, I think of you and your mother is alive again, to me. And you know that she is still there in you. Every time you look at your hand deeply you see that your hand is at the same time the hand of your mother. And if you put your hand on your forehead, it isn't only your hand touching you but the hand of your mother as well because your mother has transmitted her hand to you and that hand is still alive in you."

That is the kind of insight that we get when we know the art of looking deeply. In the practice of Buddhist meditation, when you touch the wave deeply, you touch the water. Because we are not able to touch things deeply, we qualify things as existent or non-existent. But if we can touch things deeply well we know that nothing is created nothing is destroyed.

The practice of looking deeply can give you a big release. When you are able to touch deeply what is, you can touch the world of no birth and no death. Today I want to tell our friend, that if he has the capacity of going back to himself, breathing and looking deeply he will recognize he still has many conditions for his happiness. So do his daughter and his sister. And he can continue to touch his mother and to touch his wife in his daily life because he himself is the continuation of his mother, his sister is the continuation of his mother and so is his daughter.

A few years ago when I was in London I saw in a bookstore, I saw a small book with the title, "My Mother, Myself." It is true that you are your mother, you are the continuation of your mother and this is the way of inviting you to look deeply into yourself.

CHAPTER 5

THE
INSIGHT OF
NON DUALITY

If you are a good gardener, an organic one, you know that you don't have to throw away all the garbage because you know how to transform the garbage back into vegetables. Looking into the flower, you see the sunshine, the cloud, you see the non-flower elements. Just like when you look at the tangerine what else do you see? You see the compost; you see the garbage in the flower. The flower is very fresh and beautiful and yet the garbage is in it because the gardener has used the garbage, the compost, in order to grow the flower. So you can see the presence of the garbage within the flower. That is the capacity of a person who meditates. She can see the garbage in the flower in this very moment.

Those of us who are not used to meditating, we have to wait for ten days and then, of course, the flower will become a piece of garbage. But for someone who meditates, he does not have to wait for ten days. He can see right away that the garbage is in the flower. If the flower is on its way to becoming garbage, the garbage is also on its way to becoming a flower again.

The Boddhisattvas are living beings who possess the art of transforming garbage back into flowers. A good organic gardener is not afraid of the garbage. She will not throw the garbage away. She knows that is stupid. She knows how to use the garbage in order to make compost. And the suffering in us, the pain, the anger, the jealousy, the depression in us, of course they are garbage. But if we know the practice, we will be able to transform them back into love, into joy again. We don't have to run away from our garbage, we don't have to throw away our garbage. In fact, we have to preserve it. It is thanks to it that we have joy and peace.

A true practitioner of meditation does not run. He does not try to suppress the anger, the hatred or the fear within himself. He knows how to handle these negative things in the most tender way, in the most non-violent way. This is so because he has the insight that his love is himself, his compassion is himself, his mindfulness is himself, and that his anger, too, is himself. His depression is also himself. That is why he treats negative and positive elements within him equally. That is the insight of non-duality. When you have that insight, you no longer discriminate. You no longer have the intention to fight.

To meditate does not mean to divide ourselves into two warring parties, the good side and the evil side. No. We should not transform ourselves into a battlefield, where the good fights the evil. Negative and positive, both are within us and we have to treat them equally, with non-violence, with non-discrimination. You will learn to practice mindful breathing and also embracing your irritation and anger. In Buddhism we speak of consciousness in terms of seeds, *bijas*. Our consciousness is like a piece of land containing all kinds of seeds. We have the seed of anger in our site of consciousness. We have the seed of hate, of love, of compassion, of tolerance. We have all kinds of seeds in our soil of consciousness. Call it a store of consciousness — *alaya vijnana*. That is why consciousness in Buddhism is sometime called *sarvabijata* — the totality of the seeds.

One of the seeds that is present in the depth of our consciousness is to be touched very often in our daily lives: the seed of mindfulness: *smriti* — the English word is mindfulness. Mindfulness is the capacity of being alive in the here and the now. You have the seed but because you have not watered it often it is weak. Now as we enter into a retreat, everything we do in the retreat is to touch that seed in us, to water it in order for us to renovate the energy of mindfulness. Eating we eat in mindfulness, walking we walk in mindfulness, drinking we drink in mindfulness. And we learn to do it together as a *sangha*.

CHAPTER 6

THE
FIVE SECTIONS
OF THE
TANGERINE

The tangerine symbolizes a person that is made of five elements. I will draw five sections to the tangerine.

I. THE PHYSICAL BODY

The first section of the tangerine may be called form — the physical body. Here is my body.

Breathing in I am aware of my body
Breathing out I smile through my body.

The Buddha taught us the way to contemplate the body in the body. There are many *sutras* teaching us how to go home to our bodies and reconcile our bodies because very often we are at war with our own bodies. We have made our bodies suffer because we do not live mindfully and we do not treat our bodies with non-violence, peace and love. One of the methods the Buddha proposed is for you to lie down or sit and recognize each part of your body: your head, your forehead, your eyes, your nose, your tongue, your brain, your blood, your lungs and so on. The other day I proposed:

Breathing in I am aware of my eyes
Breathing out I smile through my eyes.

This is a way to recognize one part of your body, smile through it, make peace with it and promise it that you will live in such a way that you will protect your eyes and your whole self. So when you lie down like that you begin to release all tension. You begin to focus your attention on the hair on your head.

Breathing in I am aware of the hair on my head
Breathing out I smile through it.

And then you go down, you practice scanning your body, not with laser but with another kind of light called mindfulness. You go slowly from the top of your head until you reach your heels, spend may be, half an hour or 20 minutes scanning the body like this and smile through every part of your body. This is very important.

The Buddha said, suppose there is a farmer who goes down to the cellar and brings back a bag of seeds. He opens one end of the bag and lets all the seeds fall on the floor. He identifies the various seeds: sesame seeds, corn seeds, mung beans, green beans and so on. He is able to recognize every kind of seed because he has two eyes in good condition and because he is awake.

Similarly, when you practice scanning your body, you do exactly the same: "Here are my eyes. I am smiling through my eyes." You embrace your eyes with the energy of mindfulness because the energy of mindfulness contains within itself the energy of love.

Take good care of yourself by meditation. Take good care of the body. The body is a river, and each cell of your body is a drop of water in that river. Birth and death occur every moment in that river and you do not just observe this from the outside. In true Buddhist meditation you have to remove the barriers between the observer and the object observed. You become one with your body. This is very important. An observer cannot see much. You have to be a participant. The scientists of our time understand this. When you observe an electron you cannot understand the electron. You have to participate, to become the electron. The term 'participant' is better than the term 'Observer'. You use the energy of mindfulness and you observe. You observe in such a way that you become one with the object. Your observation here is your body.

There is an old Indian image which clearly expresses this idea. A grain of salt wanted to measure the degree of salinity of the ocean. How was it to do so? There was only one way. The grain of salt jumped into the ocean and became one with the ocean. Only then can the understanding be perfect. If you cannot cross the barrier separating object and subject, then you cannot realize it. That is why in the *Satipatthana Sutra* the Buddha said: "Observe, contemplate the body in the body, contemplate the feeling in the feeling." Why that repetition? That repetition is to stress the fact that in the work of contemplation you have to become one with the object of your contemplation. When you contemplate the sunshine, if you do it well, you and the sunshine, you and the blue sky become one. All of us who have had the experience through meditation know what it is like:

Breathing in I am aware of the blue sky
Breathing out I smile through the blue sky.

And suddenly the blue sky smiles back, the blue sky becomes a smile. I become the blue sky.

2. FEELINGS

The second section of my orange is feeling. There are many kinds of feelings. To me there are at least four: pleasant

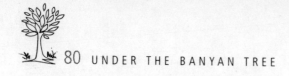

feeling, unpleasant feeling, neutral feeling and mixed feeling of pleasant and unpleasant.

When someone massages you and he presses a point, you find it both painful and pleasant at the same time. So there is such a kind of feeling that is mixed. You can experience both these different feelings at the same time. So it's not true that there are only three kinds of feelings. There are, in fact, four kinds of feelings. And this is also another river in you flowing day and night — the river of feelings. Each feeling within is a drop of water and to meditate is to sit on the bank of the river and contemplate every feeling, recognize every feeling.

When you are angry: "Breathing in I know that I am angry." You don't fight your anger. You just use the energy of mindfulness to touch your anger, to embrace your anger. You don't consider your anger as your enemy. This is the secret. You recognize every feeling that is born, that is there. You embrace it with the power or the energy of mindfulness. You take good care of that feeling and later on you look deeply into its nature. You will learn how to do it later on.

Now I would like to offer you just one example of the practice. When you have a strong emotion like fear or despair you should know how to take good care of it because it is overwhelming. At that particular point you cannot say "Present moment wonderful moment" because your emotion is so painful, so overwhelming. But you should know how to deal with that emotion. You have to learn how to embrace it because you know that in each one of us there is the seed of mindfulness. If we care to practice touching that seed everyday while walking, sitting, breathing, smiling or eating, we cultivate that energy of mindfulness. So any time you need that energy you just touch that seed of energy and suddenly that energy will be born and you can use it in order to embrace your emotion. If you succeed just once in doing so you will have peace and you will no longer be afraid of strong emotions anymore. And here is how you can do it.

When you look at a tree during a storm, you see that its branches and leaves are swaying back and forth very violently in the strong wind. You have the impression that the tree will not be able to withstand the storm. You are like that when gripped by a strong emotion. You feel that, like the tree, you too are very vulnerable. You can break any time. But if you direct your attention down to the trunk of the tree you see things differently. You see that the tree is solid and deeply rooted in the ground. If you focus your attention on the trunk of the tree you realize that, because the tree is firmly rooted in the soil, it cannot be blown away.

Similarly, each of us, in a sitting position or standing position, is like a tree. When the storm of your emotion is passing by, you should not stay in the heart of the storm which is at the level of the brain or the heart. When you are overwhelmed by strong emotions don't stay there as it is dangerous. You bring your emotion down to the level of your navel. That is the trunk, the most solid part of yourself. Those of you who practice Chinese medicine and yoga know that already. Bring your tension down a little bit below the navel and practice mindful breathing. Become aware of the rise and fall of your abdomen. In a sitting position you feel must better. Just breathe. Do not think of anything. Breathe through the movement of the rise and fall of your abdomen. Practice in this way for ten or fifteen minutes and the strong emotion will go away.

There are those of us, especially the young ones, who cannot stand strong emotions. Their suffering is so great that they believe the only way to end it is by killing themselves. That is why many young people commit suicide, because they cannot see any other way out. They do not know how to take good care of their strong emotions. But we know that an emotion is just an emotion. It comes and stays for a while and then goes away. Why do we have to die just because of one emotion? We are much more than our emotions. We have to learn this.

If during the critical moment, when the emotion is there, we know how to take refuge and where to take refuge, if we are able to breathe in and out and focus our attention on the rise and fall of our abdomen for fifteen or twenty or even twenty-five minutes, then the emotion, the storm will roll away and we will survive. And when we succeed in surviving strong emotions we experience peace. Once we have got the practice, we are no longer afraid. The next time it becomes simpler and we know that we will survive. We have to teach the young people how to do this.

If your child is in a crisis hold his hand and say: "Darling, breath in and out with me. Pay attention to the rise and fall of your abdomen." And the child, because you are there and you offer your sense of mindfulness and your solidity, he or she will be able to cross the stream of emotion. He will know that with his mother or father or big brother at his side he can survive the crisis of the strong emotion. By teaching the young people this simple practice, you might save their lives in the future. In our days there are so many young people who do not know how to handle the storm and who go and commit suicide just because of one emotion.

Of course, emotions have deep roots in us. If we know how to practice looking deeply, we will be able to uproot the painful emotions. Practicing embracing the emotions alone can be already very helpful. Meditation has two aspects: calming, stopping and then looking deeply to transform. *Samatha* is what we practice. We calm our emotions. When you have enough energy of mindfulness you can practice looking deeply into the emotion and, thereby, discover the true nature of that emotion. If you can do that then you will be able to transform the emotion.

3. PERCEPTION

The third section of the tangerine is called perception. There is a river of perception in us and each drop of water is a perception. The Buddha told us that in our daily lives we are very often victims of our wrong perceptions. A piece of rope taken to be a snake; someone who did not have the intention to make us suffer might appear as though he is trying to destroy us. We are full of wrong perceptions and that is why we suffer: wrong perceptions between father and son, mother and daughter, mother-in-law and daughter-in-law, husband and wife, wrong perceptions between friends and between nations. We suffer so much because we are victims of so many wrong perceptions and because we are too sure of our perceptions.

I know a person who was absent for one or two years and when he went home, a child was born from his wife. He suspected the child to be the son of the neighbour, because they had a very nice neighbour who often visited them and who was especially helpful when the man was away. So when he looked at the child he began to suspect that it was not his own but the neighbour's child. So he suffered very deeply, but he was too proud to tell his wife. As a result he became very cold, very distant and his wife did not know why her husband had suddenly become so distant and why he seemed to despise her. So the wife also suffered and, naturally, when husband and wife suffer the baby also suffers.

Several years later, a relative of the couple came for a visit. Looking at the little boy he exclaimed: "Oh this little boy looks exactly like his father!" Only then did the man get over his suspicion. But how much suffering had been endured by them all during those seven or eight years.

One wrong perception is enough to destroy the happiness of a whole family, of our whole life, especially when we are proud. When we suffer we don't want to confess that we suffer. We want to tell the other person that we don't need him or her. A wrong perception plus pride that is something dangerous. Are you a person who is free from that kind of suffering?

All of us have been victims of wrong perceptions and pride. If you love each other, if you claim to be a true lover, don't do like the young husband did. Because when you suffer and when you believe that the person who makes you suffer is the person you love the most in your life, you suffer one hundred times more. If another person had done that to you or had said that to you, you would have suffered less. But coming from the person that you love the most in the world it is very painful. You prefer to go into your room, lock yourself in and then cry alone rather than tell him or her that you suffer and that you need his help. You have made a wrong perception and then you cry.

In true love there is no place for pride. We know that we are human and that we can easily become victims of our wrong perceptions. That is why we have the practice of being careful of our perceptions. Always ask yourself the question, "Am I sure?" Am I sure of my perceptions?" And learn a lesson from this story. When you suffer and if you believe that your suffering has been caused by the person you love the most in the world, you have to walk up to him or to her and say, 'Darling, I suffer so much. I need your help. I don't know why you have done this." These are very simple words. It is difficult at first but you have to learn how to do it.

The next time when you suffer because you believe that the most beloved person in your life has done something to you, had said something painful to you, you have to go to him or to her, practicing mindful breathing, and ask him or her to help you. Tell him, "I suffer so much, you are the person I love the most in the world. You must help me, please explain." This will ensure that you avoid several years of suffering.

There are many of us who carry our suffering up to the grave without having had the sense to make it known to the most beloved one. That is why to meditate means to sit on the river of perception and to look deeply into each of these perceptions, recognize its presence, look deeply into it in order not to become a victim of such a perception.

4. MENTAL FORMATIONS

The fourth section of the tangerine is mental formation — *citta samskara*. According to the Mahayanist School of Vijnanavada there are about fifty one categories of mental formation — fear, hate, craving, anger, jealousy, compassion, loving kindness, mindfulness, forgetfulness, and so on. When I was a novice I had to learn all these by heart. I had to count 1, 2, 3, 4, and so on.

According to the Buddhist teachings all our mental

formations, *citta samskara*, are of an organic nature and can be transformed. The energy of anger in you can be transformed into the energy of understanding and compassion. The energy of hate in you can be transformed into the energy of tolerance and compassion. Yes, because all these mental formations are of an organic nature. Love can become hate.

Let us look at the young couple. They are about to get married. They believe very strongly that without each other, they cannot live. Sometimes they say that if they cannot marry each other then they would prefer to die. They also make that declaration very loudly: "Without you, how can I survive?" But if they do not know how to love, if they do not know how to live mindfully, then after one or two years that love can turn into hate and then they are motivated by the idea of divorce. "I cannot survive if I have to continue to live with him or her!" So they have now changed their mind completely. Love has turned into hate.

This is something that happens all the time. It is because we do not know how to nourish our love, to purify our love and transform hate into love. If love can be turned into hatred, then anger and hatred can be turned back into love. That is the optimistic message of the Buddha.

All mental formations are present in the depth of your consciousness in the form of seeds, *bijas*. Our consciousness is like the soil preserving all kinds of seeds. Every time one seed is watered, it manifests in the upper level of our mind consciousness — *manovijnana* — and becomes a mental formation. That is why in Buddhism, we call the deeper level of our consciousness, as store consciousness because it stores all kinds of seeds.

You are joyful. You are sitting and enjoying a conversation with a friend when, suddenly, someone comes and says something very mean. She has watered the seeds of anger in you. Suddenly you lose your patience. You lose your peace and become red. You shout. That is because that someone has come and touched the seed of anger in you, watered it and that seed has manifested itself into the upper level of your consciousness.

Every one of us has a seed of anger. Every one of us has a seed of compassion. We have all kinds of seeds in our store of consciousness. To practice meditation is to practice mindful watering of the seeds in us. We don't want the negative seeds to manifest often because every time a negative seed gets manifested at the base it will grow a little bit bigger. That is why let us try not to allow the negative seeds in us to be watered so often by ourselves or by the people around us: "Dear People, if you love me please refrain from watering the negative seeds in me such as anger, hatred, craving and so on. Please love me, please don't touch and water these negative seeds in me if you really care for me. And please water the positive seeds in me: the seed of tolerance, the seed of compassion, the seed of joy in me."

You have a sister who is skilful in the art of flower arrangement, Ikebana. That talent is a seed in her, a positive seed. So you come and water that seed because you see that she is not happy enough. "Dear sister how come you have not made any flower arrangement for such a long time? You know that every time you arrange a pot of flowers the whole house comes alive and becomes cheerful. Every time you arrange flowers you make all of us so happy."

So that is the way you water a positive seed in your sister. One hour later, your sister might pick up a pair of scissors and go into the garden. She will look for branches and flowers. While doing so, she waters, by herself, the seed of happiness within her. She may spend half an hour arranging a pot of flowers and during that half an hour she is practicing watering the seed of happiness in her. So to meditate is an art of mindful watering. If we love someone we should try to identify the positive seeds in him or her and try to water them often. The loved one will bloom like a flower and it is we who will profit from that happiness. Refrain from watering the negative seeds in others because if you do, you will have to suffer.

When we practice meditation, we have to take good care of each mental formation when it is manifested at the level of our mind consciousness. So mental formation is also a river, and to meditate means to be there, to recognize every mental formation that manifests, to recognize it first and then to embrace it and to look deeply into it.

5. CONSCIOUSNESS

The fifth section of the tangerine represents consciousness, *vijnana*. I would like to draw a circle here to represent our consciousness. Now I divide this circle into two and I call the upper part mind consciousness or *manovijnana*. The lower part is store consciousness or *alayavijnana*. Store consciousness is where all the seeds of mental formations are kept.

Now suppose you have a lot of pain, sorrow or fear here in the store consciousness. If these formations accept to lie down peacefully, it would be easier for us to learn. But they don't because these blocks of pain are too formed. They always try to emerge onto the upper level of our consciousness, *manovijnana*, as mental formations. We don't want them to come up but they push the door and come to settle here. Let us call mind consciousness as the sitting room and store consciousness as the basement. Anything that we don't want in the sitting room we bring it down to the basement. Many of us have important blocks of pain, of suffering in the depths of our consciousness that we cannot afford to open. We have to get busy to ensure that these guests do not come and settle in our sitting room. That is why we have to occupy the living room with other guests. Therefore we pick up a magazine or book to read, we turn on the television or we play music. We do anything in order to fill our living room with something. That is the practice of repressing. You want to set up an embargo here so that these blocks of pain have no chance to come up.

Please reflect a little. Most of us adopt this policy. We do not want to open the door for our sorrow, our fear, our depression to come up. We want to open the door to invite other things in to occupy the living room.

In the market there are plenty of things to help us in this practice. There are all kinds of entertainments. I know a refugee who belonged to the boat people category. He was able to go to America to settle after spending many years in a refugee camp in Malaysia. When he arrived with his family in America, he rented a small house and bought an old second hand television set. Television is a kind of drug. When the suffering in you is too much you cannot bear it and, in order to forget it, you need a television set.

By turning it on you fill your living room with sounds and noises. You cannot afford to be television-free. You have to create this space.

There are those of us who are strong enough to live in a television free zone, like you have non-smoking zones or non-drinking zones. In Vietnam, during the war, there was a zone called DMZ — the de-militarised zone, separating the north and the south. Now when you watch television the film or the programme is sometimes not good. It is noisy and most unpleasant. Yet you do not have the courage to turn it off. Why? Because even though it is not interesting, even though it is noisy, it is better than going home and touching the pain within yourself. That is the policy for many people in our society, not just for a few. Many of us also practice this same policy including this Vietnamese family which claims to be Buddhist.

So one day this family went to the flea market and saw a Buddha statue. They bought it for the house, but since their house is small there was no place to put the statue. So they decided to put it on the television set as it was a clean and presentable spot. It so happened that I visited them just after they had installed the Buddha. And I said: "Dear friends, this cannot go like this because these two things are poles apart. The Buddha is for us to go home to ourselves and the television is to help us run away from ourselves. These two things just cannot go together. You must remove the Buddha or you must replace the TV set with a block of stone or a brick or something like that because to me with these two things put together there is no harmony at all."

If we practice suppression in this manner, we create a situation of bad circulation of our psyche. We all know that the blood circulation is very important for our well being. If the blood does not circulate well within our bodies it gives rise to many kinds of trouble, like headaches, for example. There are tiny little veins inside the head and if the blood does not circulate well you get a headache day and night. This can be relieved by massaging your head or by taking medicine that helps to accelerate the circulation of blood. Now just as bad circulation of blood creates many problems in the body, similarly, bad circulation of the psyche also creates many mental problems. Our psyche is also a kind of blood. If that blood does not circulate well we get mental illness. If you have a depression it means that there is something blocked within your consciousness. You have psychosis.

The most meaningful transformation is that which takes place in the depth of our consciousness, called transformation at the base or *ashwayaparavriti*. You practice in such a way that not only you can see deeply in the heart of mental formation, but you can also transform the seed down there in the depth of your consciousness. And you have to ask your teacher, you have to ask your brothers and sisters, the complete ways of practice so that you can reach down and touch these seeds and help transform them. That is called transformation at the base.

We do not want our fear, our anger, our pain. We suppress it. And how do we do it? We do it by occupying our sitting room with the things provided to us by modern civilization: books, magazines, films, music. All these contain toxins. Suppose you watch one hour of television, then if you have the energy of mindfulness, then mindful TV watching can be your practice. You know that there is a lot of violence, a lot of fear and a lot of poisons in the programme of one hour. And you practice intoxicating yourself everyday. You think that you are getting relief but while entertaining yourself, you continue to bring into the depths of your consciousness more elements of pain and suffering. And the blocks of pain deep within you keep growing bigger and bigger. We intoxicate ourselves with what we consume everyday. We let our children intoxicate themselves. We don't want to be the baby-sitter of our children. We want the television set to be the baby-sitter. And our children get intoxicated everyday by what they see and they hear.

The Buddha terms these things as poisons. There are poisons in us already deep in our store consciousness and yet we are open to more poisons and toxins. Remember there were times when you spoke with a friend for one hour and after that hour of conversation you felt paralyzed because the conversation was toxic. It evoked despair, anger in you. Nowadays novelists, writers, film makers and politicians all intoxicate us. They want to foster anger and hatred in us. We listen to them because we are needy. Our environment, too, is deeply polluted by toxins and poisons. Practicing meditation means to be aware of all that is going on not only in the five elements of our body but also in the rest of the world. We are nourishing ourselves, we are feeding ourselves and our children with poisons. That is what is happening in the present moment. And if you see it, if you notice this, then that is enlightenment: enlightenment to the fact that we are intoxicating ourselves all day long. And that is why we have to find a way to stop these intoxications.

Now how do you improve the circulation of your psyche? There is a way and the way has been shown by the Buddha. If you practice mindfulness, you have enough energy in order to embrace your pain. When your anger or depression comes up, there is a zone of energy born here. The energy of anger, the energy of jealousy of hatred and of depression is there. Allow it to come up. But you should know how to take care of it. You just cannot afford to let it alone in the living room because it is devastative and destructive. You need to have the energy of mindfulness in order to embrace your pain, to embrace the energy of pain.

Breathing in I know I am angry
Breathing out I know I am taking good care of my anger.

When the baby cries, the mother rushes to the baby, of course, because the mother is there for the baby. She is working in the garden. She hears the baby cry. She knows that the baby suffers and she puts down whatever she has in her hand and goes to the baby's room and picks up the baby and holds it in her arms. This is exactly what you should do when the block of pain comes up. Using mindful breathing, you nourish mindfulness and using the energy of mindfulness you embrace your pain. You take care of it and you say, "My little anger, I know that you are there and I am taking good care of you." You do that on the insight that your anger is you. To do violence to your anger means to do violence to yourself. *Ahimsa*, non-violence, is the attitude. It is the method of embracing your pain exactly like you embrace your baby. The mother does not know what is wrong with the baby at first. But she knows that the baby suffers. That is why she picks it up and holds it dearly in her arms. A mother is made of tenderness and love. Even if the mother does not know what is the cause of the baby's suffering, the energy of tenderness and care has already begun to penetrate into the baby and the baby gets relief that is calming. That is the first part of meditation, *samatha.*

The Chinese use the word *chi*. It means 'stop', to be calm. In China, you see a lot of this sign, this script. That is the first part of meditation. Stop, be calm and embrace your pain with tenderness and compassion. If the mother continues to hold the baby tenderly like that she will be able to see the cause of the suffering of the baby very soon. The baby may have a light fever, the baby may be hungry, the diaper may be too tight. A mother is very skillful. She holds the baby in her arms. She is there and she needs to look a little bit deeply and she will find out the cause of the misery of the baby. And once she finds out the cause she will transform the situation very quickly.

Similarly, the one who meditates first embraces the pain. She can practice walking meditation holding her pain. Or she can practice sitting meditation holding her pain, like holding the baby. As she gets relief she continues to look into the nature of the pain and she will discover the true nature of the pain in terms of nutriments. Usually, when you get angry you blame your suffering on someone else: "He is the cause of all my misery. She is the cause of my misery." You blame everything on the other person. That is *avidya*, a lack of understanding.

If you know how to look deeply into the nature of your pain you see that the immediate cause, the main cause of your pain, your suffering is the seed, the negative seed within you. The other person is only the secondary cause.

You get angry so easily because the seed of anger in you is too important. Another person with the seed of anger much smaller would not get angry as easily as you do. You have practiced nourishing the seed of anger since so many years. You did not know how to take care of it, to transform it. It has continued to grow all the time and now you need only a very light stimulation for your seed of anger to manifest fully on the level of your upper consciousness. So that is the main cause.

Usually when you get angry you want to do something. You want to say something very strong, to punish the other person. You believe that by doing so you will get relief. This is very naïve. The fact is that when you have found something very strong to say to the other person he, in turn, will get angrier and will also seek release because he suffers. That is why he will find something more cruel to tell you. In that way most of you escalate your suffering and your anger all the time.

This is not wise according to the Buddha. He says "When your house is on fire you have to go home and try to put out the fire. Don't run after the person you believe to be the arsonist." But most of us do not have the capacity of going home and taking care of the fire. We always want to pursue the other person. He is the cause of my misery, you are only motivated by the desire to punish. So the practice is to go home and embrace your anger by using walking

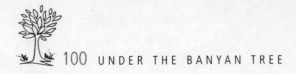

meditation, sitting meditation, mindful breathing, total relaxation, running, or jogging. You have to learn to take good care of your anger.

Next time when your partner or your child gets angry, you should help him/her to practice. Go jogging with him, sit down, or invite him for a walking meditation. Practice taking good care of the pain that is in him or her. You are there to support him and his practice.

CHAPTER 7

YOU HAVE
NO SEPARATE
EXISTENCE

In the Buddhist practice of meditation we have the practice of the emptiness of transmission. When we talk about transmission we talk about three elements: the transmitter, the one who transmits, the object that has been transmitted and the recipient, the person who receives the transmission. You have practiced this every time you take a shower. Every time you take a shower, you have a chance to look into your body and you say, this body has been transmitted to me by my parents, my ancestors. Who is the transmitter? Your parents, your ancestors have transmitted this body to you. This is the first question.

The second question, what have they transmitted to you? This body, but what is this body? The object of transmission, this body is themselves. What did they transmit to me? They transmitted themselves, because this body is the cultivation of the transmission. They do not transmit something other than themselves. Looking deeply you see that in a very scientific way. Then who is the one who receives the transmission? You, and you are one with the object of transmission.

So looking deeply you see the three ends are one — the transmitter transmits himself or herself, so the object transmitted and the transmitter they are one. The receiver also is one with the object transmitted. That is why the three are one. It is called the emptiness of transmission. Emptiness means you do not have a separate existence. All three ends are empty of a separate existence. Without the two others you cannot be yourself. Transmitter, transmitted and receiver, these three things are empty of a separate existence. The three are one. One cannot be without the two others.

Let us look now at the young person who hates his father. In our times there are many young people who hate their father or their mother and who make a very strong declaration: "I do not want to have anything to do with my father". He is too angry with his father, he suffers so much because of his father or mother. That is why he really doesn't want to have anything to do with his father. That is the desire. However, if you practice looking deeply, you see that it is not possible for you to be something different from your father. You are, and this is the hard fact, you are the continuation of your father. You are your father even if you hate your father, even if you want him to die, you want him not to exist. You are your father and that is a hard fact.

A young American came to our village in France and practiced meditation with several others. During his practice, he decided to write his father a letter, a love letter. Writing a letter is also a form of meditation practice. However, the young man could not do it, because every time he thought of his father he suffered very much. He could not afford to even think of his father, what to say of writing him a love letter. His father had already died and yet he could not reconcile with him. So I gave him an exercise which he had to practice for one week:

Breathing in I see myself as a five year old child
Breathing out I smile to that five year old
 child that was me.

When you are a five year old boy or girl you are very fragile, very vulnerable. A stern look from your father can already create a little wound in your heart. When your father says "shut up", for instance, you can get wounded. You are very tender. Sometimes you want to express yourself, you try very hard to find words and your father is a little bit irritated and he just says "shut up". It is like a bowl of cold water being poured on your heart. I see water pouring on your heart and you might be wounded deeply and the next time you will not dare to try again. That is why your communication with your father has become very difficult.

Breathing in I see myself as a five year old child
Breathing out I smile to that five year old
 child who was me.

The little boy who is deeply wounded within you, do you think that he is no longer there? The little boy/girl in you is still alive and maybe still deeply wounded. And he/she is calling for your attention. But you have no time for him. You are too busy. You think that you are entirely an adult person, but, in fact, you are still that little girl/boy that is deeply wounded. So when you breathe in and you see yourself as a little child who is fragile like that, compassion is born in your heart. And when you breathe out you smile to him/to her and that is already a smile of understanding, of compassion.

Poor little boy! He suffers so much. When he was small he was a victim of the kind of behaviour that was not his fault. A child is always very vulnerable. Even when you are just conceived by your mother, you can already begin to suffer. When the father says something unkind to the mother, when the father makes the mother suffer, you as a tiny embryo within your mother, you begin to suffer already. And that is why, if you really care for your child, even when your child is not born yet, you have to be very careful with your wife, with the mother of your child because every thing you say, every act will have an effect on the baby. Love begins, should begin very early.

There is another story of a father and his son who had behaved like enemies for more than a year. Then during one *dharma* talk, the father got enlightened. He really saw that his son was himself and that he would not have any future, his country, his people would not have any future if he was not able to reconcile with his son and restore good communication with him. So anything can happen just when you listen to a *dharma* talk, if you allow the *dharma* to penetrate into the soil of your store consciousness. The best way to listen to the *dharma* talk is to not use your intellect. To use your intellect in order to judge, to comment is like using a piece of nylon in order to cover the ground to prevent the rain water from seeping into the soil. Thus the rain fails to sink deeply into the soil and touch the seed of understanding that is already there in the soil.

Our consciousness, our store consciousness is the land, the soil. There are so many seeds inside, the seed of understanding, the seed of enlightenment and so on. When we listen to a *dharma* talk, we allow it to penetrate like rain into our soil. If the seed of understanding is moistened by the rain, it will sprout and the flower of understanding will grow. So in the time of the Buddha from time to time, there was a person who during the *dharma* talk given by the Buddha would get enlightened. The Buddha always noticed the presence of such persons by the way he or she would look. For example, during the first *dharma* talk he gave in the deer park in Benares, one of the five disciples while listening to the first *dharma* talk about the form of the truth, got enlightened and the Buddha knew this at once and he said: "Kondanya, you have understood, you have seen it." An immaculate vision of the *dharma* was born in Kondanya. It is recorded like that in the first *dharma* talk given by the Buddha at the Deer park.

So the man at the retreat got the vision, that enlightenment during the *dharma* talk. He went home crying with the strong intention of restoring communication between him and his son. He did not do much, he just silently hugged his son and the message got across. And the next morning the mother of the young man was very surprised to see, across the breakfast table, father and son, talking to each other. This had not happened since more than one year.

So all of us have the power to change the situation, if we care to practice mindful walking, mindful breathing to encourage the energy of mindfulness and to practice looking deeply to understand. Because understanding when it comes, will liberate us. It will help us to get rid of our anger, our hate and so on. And love is something that can only be born on the ground of understanding. *Prajna* and *karuna*, there are two words but they point to the same reality. Where there is understanding, *prajna*, there is love. Where there is true love *maitri* and *karuna*, there already exists *prajna* or understanding. Where there is no understanding, there is no true love. It is called craving, desire or something like that. True love is made of understanding. And when understanding is there, there is no place for pride and arrogance. To cultivate the energy of loving kindness is also our practice, because without loving kindness, without compassion in us, there is no way that we can relate to other people, to the world, and we will continue to be cut off and we will continue to suffer.

Samyojana is a Sanskrit term. It means an internal formation. It may be an attachment. It may be a block of pain in us. When you say something or when you do something to another person which causes him or her to suffer, then an internal knot is created within her consciousness, that is called a *samyojana*. Out of our unskillfulness, living without mindfulness we make mistakes in our daily life and we create knots of suffering in the person we love. We don't want her to suffer, and yet we make her suffer. And we continue to repeat that kind of unskillfulness so the block of suffering grows a little bit bigger each time. If we continue like that, one day the suffering will be too big and communication will become difficult.

All of us wish to have good health, to have success, and to have good relationship with the main people in our life. We know that these three elements are essential to our happiness and most of us suffer deeply when our relationship with the other person gets worse. Then when communication is no longer possible, the suffering reaches its highest point. When the father is no longer capable of talking to his son, when the husband is no longer capable of talking to his wife, the suffering really becomes too great. There are people who suffer so much that they become very tense. They look like a bomb ready to explode. Look at them. You don't recognize them. They do not look very different from a bomb. Such a person's partner, his children are afraid of him/of her, not because they want to boycott him but because they are afraid of suffering more. When someone suffers so much and does not know how to transform that suffering, he/she will naturally spill the suffering all over inside. And it is the people who live around him or her that have to bear that suffering.

You don't dare to approach that person because you are afraid of suffering. It's not because you want to despise him or to boycott him but because you want to keep a distance from him. He believes that you despise him, you want to kick him out of your life and he suffers more. According to the teachings of the Buddha, it is possible for you to help him to suffer less. You can help to diffuse the bomb within him. You need to be a Boddhisatva in order to be able to diffuse the bomb in such a person. And this can be done with the practice of mindfulness.

CHAPTER 8

WALKING
MEDITATION

During the four days we are together you are requested to practice walking mindfully not only for your sake, but for all of us, because the collective energy is extremely important. Please walk as if you have arrived already. Your true form is in the here and the now. Why continue to run? I am a person who is able to walk mindfully all day. Whether it is on the soil of India or France or Germany, it is my home. I have arrived. I am home. I don't have to run anymore. Every step generates peace and joy. And when people see me walking like that they have confidence. They go back to themselves and they learn to walk like me, touching peace, touching joy that is available in their own consciousness. When we see you walking and enjoying every step like that, we have a chance to go back to ourselves and we will walk like you.

In North America, from time to time, we have a retreat of two thousand, three thousand people. And when you practice walking meditation you can see two thousand, three thousand people walking mindfully, touching the earth with joy, with peace, with love. And it provides a very powerful collective energy that penetrates into each of us. It is possible to transform this very land into the land of peace. Everyday we practice walking meditation together and the rest of the day every time we need to go from one place to another, no matter how short that distance, we always practice walking meditation. I always do this. Within a retreat or outside the retreat, I always do this.

Why do I have to run? I am at peace with myself. I am at peace with everything else. I experience the joy of *aparahita*, aimlessness. I don't have any aim. I don't run after anything. I have practiced stopping. And when you have stopped, you will have insight and the insight will liberate you. *Samatha* is very important. *Vipassana* will not be possible without *Samatha*. *Vipassana* means deeply. If you don't stop how can you look deeply? If you do not stop the thinking, the worry, the hatred, the blaming, how can you look into the nature of the tangerine and see the cosmos in a tangerine?

We have many ways of walking, and enjoying our walking. You may like to use a short poem. In France, I teach the French children to use the word *oui* and *merci*. When I practice with French children I advise them to breathe in and to make two steps. I tell them, " when you touch the ground with your feet, you say *oui*" which means 'yes' *oui*, yes. Children like to say no, so you have to teach them how to say 'yes' to things.

There are many things to say 'yes' to. The blue sky; "Would you like to say yes to the blue sky? "Yes.". You say 'yes' to the sunshine, to the green vegetation, to the clean air, to the water, to mother earth. There are so many positive things that are there. And if we do not know how to say 'yes' to them and protect them, they will go away. Trees will die if we don't know how to appreciate them when they are still

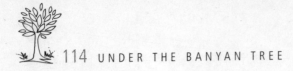

alive. Trees are being cut down, they are dying, and if we don't show our capacity of appreciating them when they are green, solid, refreshing, we will not do anything in order to preserve them and we will lose them very soon.

That is why it is our practice to say 'yes' to everything that is positive around us and inside of us. 'Yes!' That is awareness. Yes! Yes! And when you pick up your foot you say 'thanks, thanks'. The French children say *merci, merci — oui, oui, merci*. And walking back and forth for about three minutes they stop, they touch the blue sky, they listen to the birds, they recognize the wonders of life while maintaining mindful breathing.

Breathing in, the sky is so blue.
Breathing out, I smile at the blue sky.
Breathing in, the birds are singing
Breathing out I smile to the blue sky.

You practice mindful breathing in order to keep the object of your mindfulness present. If you stop practicing mindful breathing, your thinking mind starts to think and you lose everything. I think, therefore, I am not there.

To meditate does not mean to think. It means to be, to be yourself, to be the sky, the blue sky, to be the birds, to be the trees, to be life that manifests itself in the present moment. We have to love. In a retreat we have to be born again. In our spiritual life we have to learn how to breathe again. We have to learn how to walk again. Like a baby, we have to learn how to sit again.

Mindfulness helps us to be born again and to be really alive, so that we can live out every minute, every moment of our daily life, in the deepest way. To meditate does not mean to run away from life or to be cut off from reality. To meditate is to make a return, to make a comeback. It is to go back and to touch life deeply, to arrive. You have arrived in the present moment. To arrive, please remember, is in the here and the now. Because it is only in the here and the now that life is available. To walk, to practice walking meditation as such is to walk without the intention to arrive if we are to use the word arrival. We have arrived in the here.

Talking about destination, we should ask why we are always in a hurry to arrive. What is our destination? What is our final aim? Our final destination is our own death, it is the crematory. Why do we have to hurry to go there? I don't want to go in the direction of death. I only want to go in the direction of life. And what is the direction? It is the present moment because life, the address of life, is the present moment. It is easy to remember that address and you can reach it as quickly as an e-mail or a fax. Because

as soon as you dial with your mindful breathing, you will already be there.

The moment you begin breathing in and out mindfully, you arrive. The moment you touch the ground with your foot mindfully, you are already home. That is why I suggest that when you make two steps you say, "I have arrived, I have arrived." And when you are tired you make another two steps and you say "I am home, I am home.", because my home is the here and the now. Thus you learn the art of stopping by walking.

Angulimala — remember him? He was the one who ran after the Buddha in order to kill him. And the Buddha was walking in the walking meditation style peacefully. Angulimala caught hold of him shouting: "Stop, monk, stop!" The Buddha didn't stop. He continued to walk peacefully and Angulimala had to run after him. Running along with the Buddha he said: "Monk I told you to stop, why did you not stop?"

The Buddha replied: "Angulimala I have stopped a long time ago. It is you who has not stopped."

This is a powerful statement and Angulimala was very intelligent. His question was answered by the Buddha in just one sentence.

CHAPTER 9

EATING
MINDFULLY

Sometimes I sit quietly and enjoy the togetherness of the *sangha* and also share anew with the monks and the nuns who wear the *sangati* robes. Today you can have an idea of how monks ate in the old times. They carried their bowl and they ate out of their personal bowl, mindful of every morsel of food they ate.

When you sit down, sit mindfully and enjoy your position of sitting and allow yourself to be penetrated by the calm and energy of mindfulness and joy of the *sangha*, the collective joy and happiness of the *sangha*. Let it penetrate into you. Open yourself. Before we eat we already practice being there to offer the *sangha* our true presence. Be there one hundred percent. Do not allow yourself to be caught in your worries and projects. Be there like a flower for the rest of the *sangha* and you will see that you will receive a lot of positive energy from everyone.

Then we begin with the five contemplations. It has been practiced for many thousands of years. Before eating someone will read aloud the five contemplations so that we can contemplate on them together. When we pick up something like a carrot or a green bean, look at it, smile to it so that it will reveal itself to you as a wonderful presence. For the piece of carrot or the green bean is also am ambassador from the cosmos. It contains within itself everything for your nourishment and growth.

When you have seen it in that light, put it into your mouth, only that and not other things like projects, worries or thoughts. When you chew, chew mindfully. It is wonderful to chew a piece of food like that. It becomes a source of joy and peace.

In the Catholic Church they celebrate the Eucharist. They receive a piece of bread representing the flesh of the person of Jesus Christ, the body of Jesus Christ. In the Buddhist practice of eating, each morsel of food contains the universe. It is the body of the cosmos and you are getting touch with the wonders of life through that piece of food. So chew it with joy. Enjoy the food that has been offered to you. If you eat it mindfully, you deserve eating that food.

You eat in such a way that compassion and joy become possible. From time to time you stop and you look at the *sangha*, at one member of the *sangha*, to realize that to be with the *sangha*, to share anew is also great happiness. We do this exactly as it was done in the time of the Buddha. We take time to eat our food. You may like to chew thirty times before you swallow. It would be very tasty if you care to chew like that. It will also bring happiness.

You may need forty-five minutes if you eat like that. But if you eat too quickly then you have to sit until the end because this is the formal meal. So just enjoy chewing your food slowly. Everyone will be there to support you.

Eat in such a way that peace and joy and happiness become possible in the here and the now.

In Plum Village, although we don't wear the ceremonial *sangati* everyday, we do eat like this everyday. So enjoy your formal meal today.

CHAPTER 10

EXERCISES
FOR
DAILY PRACTICE

1. THE MANTRA FOR BRINGING JOY AND HARMONY OF BODY AND MIND

Dear friends, when you smile about 300 muscles on your face become relaxed. Look at someone who is angry or afraid or fearful. Their face is very tense. We know that there are something like 300 muscles on our face and when you get angry all of them become very tense and the nervous system behind it gets very tense as well. But if we know how to breathe in and smile, suddenly all the tension will go very quickly. And you will look much better, more presentable to the world.

When you are on your cushion practicing breathing in and out, enjoy and smile. Smile to yourself. The object of your smile is yourself. It is a smile of compassion. Go back and smile to yourself. In the dark when you practice sitting meditation please practice the smile. Breathing in you relax, breathing out you smile.

I would like to offer you a very short *mantra*, for the practice of breathing in and out, when you sit or when you walk. It is very simple and you can use it for a long time.

Breathing in I know I am breathing in.
Breathing out I know I am breathing out.

And we make it short: *in, out.*

That is the first part of the exercise and you may like to practice it for a few minutes. Just pay attention to your incoming breath and the outgoing breath. Enjoy your in-breath and your out-breath. And then later on you will switch into the second part of the *mantra*.

Breathing in I notice that my in-breath has become
*   deeper*
Breathing out I notice that my out-breath has become
*   slower.*

You don't have to use all the words. You just say *deep, deep, slow slow.*

In this part of the exercise, you do not make an attempt to make your in-breath deeper or your out-breath slower. After having breathed in and out for sometime your in-breath will naturally become deeper, without your having to make any effort. And of, course your out-breath will become slower. It only means that you notice that the quality of your breathing has improved. You don't make any effort. Just enjoy your in-breath and out-breath, and after three or five times like that, naturally your in-breath and out-breath will become deeper and slower. It is more pleasant. It will bring joy and harmony into your body and your mind.

Therefore we use only two words, '*deep*' and you enjoy it, '*slow*' and you enjoy it. You might practice it sitting in the bus, in the train, even while driving or cooking your meals. Smile. Your meditation for everywhere is: *in, out, deep, slow.*

Later on you switch into the third part of the exercise.

Calmly breathing in, I calm my body. Breathing out I take it at ease, I ease everything. Nothing is important. Nothing is as important as my peace. Peace is the most important thing so I take everything at ease and establish peace and harmony within myself.

Breathing in I feel calm
Breathing out I feel peace.
— Breath

In the *anapanasati sutra,* the *sutra* on mindful breathing, the Buddha suggested:

Breathing in I calm activities of my body.
Breathing out I calm the activities of my body
— Physical formation

And then later on he suggests:

Breathing in I calm the activities of my mind
Breathing out I calm the activities of my mind
— Mental formation

In meditation, three elements become one — body, mind and breath, whether it is in the sitting position or standing position or lying position or walking position. The three things become one because you are in *samadhi*. You are concentrated. Concentration means the oneness of body and mind and breath. And when the three have become one, what happens in one will happen also in the two others. If your breath becomes more harmonious and more peaceful, your mind will do likewise and so also your body. When you bring some peace and stability to your body, it means you bring it also to your breath and to your mind.

In order to arrive at the state of oneness of body and mind, you don't need a lot of time. Breathing in and out once or twice will be enough to bring body and mind together, united with the breath. What you have got then is the first fruit of meditation, the oneness of body and mind. Suddenly you are there.

Breathing in I feel calm. This world of mine means breath, body and mind at the same time, because we know in meditation that the three elements become one. Breathing out I feel ease within myself, I feel at peace with myself, and I bring that peace into my body, into my mind by practicing my full breathing.

Breathing in, breathing out I have to release. To release means to let go of whatever is there: my tensions, my projections, my concerns, my desires, my fear. *I allow them to go. I am not trying to grasp, to cling on to them. Breathing in I smile.* You are smiling at yourself. This is the smile of freedom. You have recovered your sovereignty, you have reclaimed your liberty as a free human being. You are not a victim of anything including your fears and your doubts. This smile is strengthening, this smile is to restore yourself, to restore your sovereignty. *Nothing is important except my peace, my freedom.* So this smile is a smile of someone who has walked the path. *Nothing is as important as my peace, my freedom.* So you have to smile and breathe.

I repeat: *in out, deep, slow, calm, ease, smile, release.*

And the last part of the exercise: *present moment, wonderful moment.*

This is because you have got enlightenment, the enlightenment that you are there, arrived and that you are touching life in that moment. That is the object of your enlightenment. And you see that to be alive is to be touching life in this present moment and it is a wonderful thing. That is why when you breathe out you smile and you say "wonderful moment."

Of course there are moments that are difficult. You cannot term them as wonderful. But even so in difficult moments we have to be really there in order to take care of these moments. Not only happiness is wonderful but the suffering is also wonderful. You will find out later on that not only life is wonderful but death, too, is wonderful. You cannot separate life from death, for death is a part of life. Life is made of non-life elements, including death. Like the biologist, you know already that the dying self is very crucial for other selves. We undergo death at every moment of our daily life, at the level of the body and also of the mind. There is also something dying in this very moment, in order to make life possible, in order to enable it to continue.

You must sing this *mantra* and remember to learn it by heart because it is a very wonderful *mantra* for bringing joy and harmony into your body and mind.

2. THE MANTRA FOR THE
PRACTICE OF MINDFUL LIVING

I will sing this *mantra* for it is easier to remember and to learn by heart if you are going to use it day and night for the practice of mindful living.

Breathing in I smile
Breathing out I smile.

To smile is to restore yourself, to restore your serenity and to be able to accept my peace. So this smile is a smile of someone who has won the battle. *Nothing is as important as my peace, my freedom.* So you let go, smile. Live.

I repeat:

In, out, deep, slow, calm, ease, smile, release.

Then the last part of the exercise — *present moment, wonderful moment,* — because you have got enlightenment, enlightenment that you are there, and that you are touching life in the present moment. That is the object of your enlightenment.

I will sing this *mantra* for then it is easier to remember, to learn by heart, because it is a very wonderful *mantra* if you are going to use it day and night for the practice of mindful living.

(sings)

In, out, deep, slow, peace, love, calm, ease, smile, release, present moment, wonderful moment

These are the abbreviations of the *mantra*. I repeat the *mantra* again.

Breathing in I know that I am breathing in
Breathing out I know that I am breathing out
Breathing in I notice that my in-breath has become deep
Breathing out I notice that my out-breath
    has become slow
Breathing in I feel calm
Breathing out I feel at ease
Breathing in I smile
Breathing out I release
Breathing in I establish myself in the present moment
Breathing out I know this is a wonderful moment.

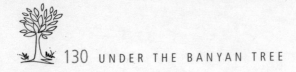

If someone asks you to see whether the best moment of your life has arrived or not, the best moment of my life, has it arrived? No it does not seem that the best moment of my life has arrived you say, but I believe that it will arrive soon and there is a belief that it will arrive soon. But we know very well that if you continue to live exactly as you have in the last twenty years, then even in the next twenty years it will not arrive. The Buddha is very smart on this. He said, "You have to transform this present moment into the best moment of your life." The best moment of your life is now or never. And how can you make the present moment into the best moment of your life without being there completely body and mind united with your smile, and your relaxation? Is there anything important, more important than your peace, your smile, and a harmony within you? Why do you have to sacrifice these things for other things? What are the other things, money, fame, wealth? They are not worth it. So the fine things, the best things of your life are solidity, freedom, peace, stability.

3. MEDITATION ON REALITY

These eyes are not me
I am not caught by these eyes
I am life without boundaries
I have never been born
and I will never die.

This body is not me
I am not bound by this body
I am life without boundaries
I have never been born and
I will never die.

Look at the ocean and mountains,
Look at the sky filled with stars
All are manifestations of my wonderous mind
My son and my daughter,
My children, my grandchildren,
My friends, my realisations...............
All are manifestations of my wonderous mind

Since immemorial time I have been free
Birth and death are only a threshold
By which I passed by
Birth and death are just a hide and seek game

So laugh at me, smile with me,
Let us say goodbye
Say goodbye till we meet again
We will meet today, we will meet tomorrow
You will meet at every walk of life

So laugh with me, smile with me
Hold my hand, let us say goodbye
Say goodbye till we meet again
We will meet today, we will meet tomorrow
You will meet at each walk of life...

ABOUT **THICH NHAT HANH**

Thich Nhat Hanh is a Vietnamese Buddhist monk, poet, and tireless worker for peace. He leads a meditation community in southwestern France, and he is author of more than eighty-five books in English. His life-long efforts to generate peace and reconciliation moved Martin Luther King, Jr. to nominate him for the Nobel Peace Prize in 1967. He is the founder of Van Hanh Buddhist University in Saigon, and has taught at Columbia University and the Sorbonne.

The Path of Emancipation
by Thich Nhat Hanh

In May 1998, more than four hundred practitioners from around the world joined Thich Nhat Hanh's first 21-day retreat in North America in Vermont to experience mindfulness. The Path of Emancipation, which transcribes this retreat, comprises an in-depth instruction in the 'Sixteen Ways of Breathing" from the Discourse on the full Awareness of Breathing. When Thich Nhat Hanh discovered this discourse, he said, "I felt I was the happiest person in the world."

Applying the teachings to everyday life, Thich Nhat Hanh shows how it is possible to slow down and get in touch with our breathing. He teaches the practice of mindful breathing, walking, and sitting and how the practice of mindfulness releases suffering and leads to a wholesome and happy life.

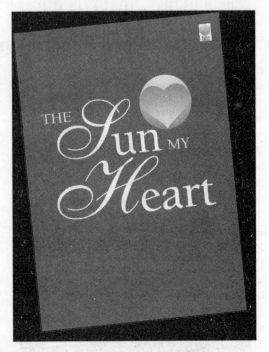

From *FULL CIRCLE*

OLD PATH WHITE CLOUDS
by Thich Nhat Hanh

Old Path White Clouds presents the life and teachings of Gautama Buddha. Drawn directly from 24 Pali, Sanskrit, and Chinese sources, and retold by Thich Nhat Hanh in his inimitably beautiful style, this book traces the Buddha's life slowly and gently over the course of 80 years, partly through the eyes of Svasti, the buffalo boy, and partly through the eyes of the Buddha himself. **Old Path White Clouds** is destined to become a classic of religious literature.

Other Books by **Thich Nhat Hanh**
published by **FULL CIRCLE** & **HIND POCKET BOOKS**

The Stone Boy

Being Peace

Present Moment
Wonderful Moment

Transformation &
Healing

The Heart of
Understanding

Cultivating the
Mind of Love

Our Appointment with Life

Teachings on Love

Interbeing

Breathe!
You Are Alive!

The Long Road
Turns to Joy

Dharmacharya Shantum Seth, ordained by
Thich Nhat Hanh, offers teachings and shares the
practice of Mindfulness in different parts of India
and the world. He also leads pilgrimages
'In the Footsteps of the Buddha'.
Please visit: www.buddhapath.com

Practitioners of Mindfulness Meditation meet
regularly at different locations in India to meditate
and deepen their understanding of the Dharma.
Please visit: www.ahimsatrust.org If you would like
to attend please write to ahimsa.trust@gmail.com

For worldwide contacts and teachings of
Thich Nhat Hanh, please visit www.plumvillage.org

FULL CIRCLE publishes books on inspirational subjects, religion, philosophy, and natural health. The objective is to help make an attitudinal shift towards a more peaceful, loving, non-combative, non-threatening, compassionate and healing world.

FULL CIRCLE continues its commitment towards creating a peaceful and harmonious world and towards rekindling the joyous, divine nature of the human spirit.

Our fine books are available at all leading bookstores across the country.

FULL CIRCLE *PUBLISHING*

Editorial Office

J-40, Jorbagh Lane, New Delhi-110003
Tel: 24620063, 24621011 • Fax: 24645795
E-mail: fullcircle@vsnl.com • website: www.atfullcircle.com

Bookstores

5B, Khan Market, New Delhi - 110003
Tel: 24655641/2/3

N-8, Greater Kailash Part I Market, New Delhi - 110048
Tel: 29245641/3/4

Number 8, Nizamuddin East Market,
New Delhi - 110013

Join the

WORLD
WISDOM BOOK CLUB

GET THE BEST OF WORLD LITERATURE
IN THE COMFORT OF YOUR HOME AT
FABULOUS DISCOUNTS!

Benefits of the Book Club

Wherever in the world you are, you can receive the best of books at your doorstep.

- Receive FABULOUS DISCOUNTS by mail or at the **FULL CIRCLE** Bookstores in Delhi.
- Receive Exclusive Invitations to attend events being organized by **FULL CIRCLE**.
- Receive a FREE copy of the club newsletter — The World Wisdom Review — every month.
- Get UP TO 25% OFF.

Join Now!

It's simple. Just fill in the coupon overleaf and mail it to us at the address below:

FULL CIRCLE
J-40, Jorbagh Lane, New Delhi-110003
Tel: 24620063, 24621011 • Fax: 24645795

Y es, I would like to be a member of the

World Wisdom Book Club

Name ☐ Mr ☐ Mrs ☐ Ms...

Mailing Address...

....

....

City................................... Pin.......................................

Phone.................................. Fax.......................................

E-mail...

Profession............................... D.O.B..............................

Areas of Interest..

....

Mail this form to:
The World Wisdom Book Club
J-40, Jorbagh Lane, New Delhi-110003
Tel: 24620063, 24621011 •Fax: 24645795

UNDER THE BANYAN TREE